EVOLUTION OF COMMAND AND CONTROL DOCTRINE

FOR

CLOSE AIR SUPPORT

by

Riley Sunderland

OFFICE OF AIR FORCE HISTORY

HEADQUARTERS, UNITED STATES AIR FORCE

March 1973

FOREWORD

This study was prepared in response to an Air Staff request for a history of command and control procedures used in close air support (CAS). The writer, Mr. Riley Sunderland, is co-author of the official Army history of the China-Burma-India Theater, World War II, and wrote 5 RAND Corp. studies of the Communist insurgency in Malaya. He begins with brief comment on the invention of close air support during World War I, then moves on to the evolution of the modern Tactical Air Control System (TACS) from the late 1930's to the present. Only major developments are treated to keep the subject manageable.

The author, distinguishing between doctrine and procedure, has focused on the former. For official definitions of "doctrine" and "close air support," the reader is referred to Air Force Manual (AFM) 11-1, USAF Glossary of Standardized Terms.

Close air support is the third of 3 principal missions of tactical air forces, of which air superiority is first and interdiction second. The classic statement is in War Department Field Manual (FM) 100-20, Command and Employment of Air Power, 21 July 1943, paragraph 16. Close air support may also be provided by strategic air, e.g., St. Lo, France, 1944; Khe Sanh, South Vietnam, 1968. The responsible air commander must weigh the allocation of resources between the 3 basic tactical air missions, lest an injudicious commitment of his forces to any one mission degrades his ability to perform the others. As will be seen in Mr. Sunderland's narrative, this has been a major issue in the handling of tactical air.

BRIAN S. GUNDERSON
Brigadier General, USAF
Chief, Office of Air Force History

CONTENTS

FOREWORD ii

LIST OF ILLUSTRATIONS vi

PART I. WORLD WAR I TO VIETNAM, 1916-1961 1

    The Germans Introduce Modern Close Air Support 3
    Command and Control of Close Air Support,
        Luftwaffe, 1940 4
    The French System Contrasted 6
    The United States Begins to Adapt to Modern War 7
    Early Combat Experience in the Pacific, Aug-Oct 1942 ... 10
    The Tunisian Lessons 11
    Publishing a Charter for Tactical Air 13
    The Theaters Find a Way to Control
        "Contact Zone Missions" 15
    Close Air Support Prepares the Normandy Breakout 18
    The Lessons of World War II: FM 31-35 21
    The Doctrinal Background to Korea: TACS 25
    Korea Confirms FM 31-35 on TACS 27
    The First Days in Korea: CAS without TACS 28
    Weighing the Korean Experience 31
    Doctrinal Trends on the Eve of Vietnam 32

PART II. SOUTH VIETNAM, 1962-1969 36

    Setting Up the TACS in South Vietnam 37
    The Problem of the Immediate Air Request Net 38
        The Air-Ground Request Net 39
        The New Air Request Net 40
    Developments Within CONUS Affecting Doctrine 42
    Adjusting the Vietnam TACS to Accommodate
        Large USA/USMC Units 44
    I Corps Buildup Plus Marine Air
        Causes Control Problems 46
    "Single Manager" in Operation 47
    The Parallel DASC's in II Corps 49
    The FAC's Roles and Missions Expand, 1965-1969 53
    Command and Control of CAS Affects a Battle:
        Duc Lap, 1968 55

SUMMARY 58

FOOTNOTES 61

GLOSSARY 69

LIST OF ILLUSTRATIONS

Figure		Page
1	Command Relationship, North Africa............	22
2	Command Relationship, Western Desert Campaign	22
3	Air-Ground Operations System	23
4	Typical Tactical Air Control System	24
5	Immediate Air Request Net	41
6	Preplanned Request System	50
7	Immediate Air Requests	51

I. WORLD WAR I TO VIETNAM
1916 - 1961

Massed combat aviation under unified control was introduced by the Royal Flying Corps (RFC) at the Battle of the Somme, 1916. A year later in November 1917, the RFC with the British Army introduced close air support by massed aviation at the Battle of Cambrai. Two hundred and eighty-nine aircraft, of which 134 were fighters, were opposed by only 78 German planes. The fighters flew from dawn to dusk, using machine guns and 25-lb. bombs. The combination of massed air and massed armor was a stunning surprise. A few days later, the counterattacking Germans used close air support for the first time against British infantry; their British targets were as surprised and demoralized by the novel attack as the Germans had been.

In March 1918 massed close air support by the RFC was effective in helping plug the gaps torn in the British lines by the great German offensive. At one moment, some 100 British fighters were aloft covering the threatened flank of the British Third Army. On occasion, British fighters actually repelled German infantry attacks. Gen. Erich Ludendorff, the German Chief of Staff, described the losses of German infantry to air attacks as "'extraordinarily high.'"

By the 8th of August 1918, later termed by Ludendorff the black day of the German Army, the Royal Air Force (RAF)--successor to the Flying Corps--could offer close air support on a scale respectable even by today's standards. In the first 36 hours of the action, RAF fighters expended 122,150 rounds of ammunition and 1,562 25-lb bombs.

Command and control of the fighters was simple but effective. Each field army had an aircraft brigade headquarters allocated to it and the brigade, in turn, had a fighter wing. RAF headquarters shifted fighter and bomber squadrons from one brigade to another as it assessed the situation. Observation was the work of squadrons dedicated to army corps. Communication with the infantry and tanks was rudimentary. Contact patrols watched for the display of panels, lights, or smoke by the infantry. Visual signals linked air and armor; radio experiments were highly promising as the war was ending.[1]

Entering World War I with an embryonic air force, the Americans borrowed ideas from the French and British. They too had observation squadrons assigned to each corps "at the direct orders of the corps commander."[2] There was unified control in that Gen. John J. Pershing's U.S. First Army had a single Air Service, finally under Brig. Gen. William Mitchell. Though Mitchell was subordinate to Pershing, in practice the relation was that of a theater commander to his air force component commander/tactical air force commander. Perhaps because Mitchell was subordinate to Pershing, his headquarters and Pershing's were collocated, unlike the British practice. However, Mitchell's memoirs suggest he saw the advantages of collocation. Finally, he enthusiastically adopted the idea of massed close air support that Marshal of the Royal Air Force Viscount Trenchard had developed for the RAF and used it at St. Mihiel and in the Meuse-Argonne. Air-ground liaison was handled as did the British, though Mitchell later recalled arranging for a number of radios to be issued to the infantry in the hope that they would keep in touch. In default of formal organization for liaison, they did not.[3]

Meanwhile, on their side of the lines the Germans did not keep pace with the Allies in the use of close air support, but paralleled them in unified control of air power and surpassed them in one important aspect of the command and control of close air support by inventing the air liaison officer (ALO) and coming close to the tactical air control party (TACP). They attached ALO's to infantry divisions in the area of main offensive effort. Their task was to keep the air up to date on the ground situation (particularly where the front was), on the intent and plans of the Army, on important targets within the battle area, and on the current air situation. If circumstances required, the ALO's were given radios with operators to make them independent of insecure wire links.[4]

The state of close air support and its associated command and control at the end of World War I may be indicated graphically:

	British	German	American
First use of CAS	1917	1917	1918
Unified control	1916	1916	1918
Massing of squadrons	1916	?	1918
Collocated headquarters	No	No	1918
Air liaison officers	No	1918	No

Plainly, the principles of correct employment of combat aviation were not self-evident. Close air support was not discovered until after 3 years of heavy fighting; unified control and massing of assets at the critical point took 2 years. With the exception of aerial observation, which was used from the beginning of World War I, similar comment might be made on any point of air doctrine. Experience, observation, reflection, discussion, staffing, decision, training, implementation, fresh experience all took time and finally the results were distilled into the fairly terse statements of doctrine.

The Germans Introduce Modern Close Air Support

On 10 May 1940 the armed forces of the Third Reich began moving west into Holland, Luxembourg, and Belgium. To meet them, the British and French forces swung east like a gate hinged west of the Ardennes Forest near Sedan. The French Ninth Army, a reserve formation, had the southern part of the hinge along the Meuse. The 12th of May, as it was occupying position, its staff and commanders became aware of powerful German elements closing on the Meuse. They interpreted German intent in the light of French practice in mounting a river crossing, which required several days. They therefore husbanded artillery ammunition and did not start requests for air support up through the slow, cumbersome net (see below, p 6). As late as the morning of the 13th, local commanders said they did not need close air support. No word went to the RAF.

At 0700 on the 13th, the German air bombardment of the French defenses along the Meuse above Sedan got under way. The first hint that air cover might be needed came from General Billotte, commanding the French 1st Army Group, and the officer through whom requests had to pass to l'Armee de l'Air* from the troops along the Meuse. It was a simple request that first priority for air action be given to the Sedan area. Meanwhile, the German bombing from hundreds of massed aircraft grew heavier and reached its peak at 1200. The defenders felt exposed and alone. Bunkers, artillery positions, communications, trenches were hammered.

The German crossing of the Meuse began about 1500. The French infantry began to panic. By nightfall the Germans had their bridgehead, a substantial part of the French infantry had vanished, and both the French corps and division artillery were erroneously reporting German armor near their command posts (CP's). The panic was on, German armored and motorized divisions had their breakthrough, and the Germans would defeat France, Belgium, Holland, Luxembourg, and a British expeditionary force in 6 weeks.[5]

Here one must note the impact on tactics of electronic technology or, in 1940, the lack of what today one takes for granted. In 1939-1940 there was no battlefield radar. Consequently, the side that took the initiative and massed its tactical air had a great advantage over opponents who necessarily relied on radio intercepts and visual/aural indications for early warning. The state of flight control can be imagined. As will be noted, French command arrangements did nothing to compensate.

<u>Command and Control of Close Air Support, Luftwaffe, 1940</u>

Behind the German successes of May-June 1940 lay a system of command and control of close air support that, in sharp distinction to the diffused, lethargic Allied effort, could produce the following order to the German 1st Panzer Division for the Meuse crossing:[6]

---
*"French Air Force" does not convey the meaning of the original. It was a parallel organization to the French Army and was the French Army of the Air.

> On the 13th of May the point of main effort
> [original emphasis] of our Western Offensive lies
> in the sector of Group von Kleist [i.e., Panzergruppe
> von Kliest with 800 tanks and a motorized corps].
> Almost the whole of the German air force (sic) will
> support this operation.

German doctrine for command and control of close air support--evolved in inter-war doctrinal studies and combat experiences in the Spanish Civil War and the 1939 Polish campaign--provided unified control, collocated air-ground headquarters, air liaison officers and TACP's at the point of main effort; and a fast air request net linking army corps with their associated fliegerkorps.* The Luftwaffe itself was designed to support the German Army as a vast tactical air force. Its 3 basic missions were the classic ones cited above. It was equipped and organized accordingly. This singleness of purpose made it highly effective in France and Poland in 1939-1940 but much less so in the Battle of Britain immediately thereafter.[7]

Parallel, collocated air and ground elements were:

CINC Army	A Luftwaffe general
Army Group	Tactical air support headquarters
Army	Tactical air support headquarters
Corps	ALO
Division	ALO

Requests went from battalion or regiment, or artillery unit, through division to corps. Corps could approve, redraft, or disapprove. Corps and fliegerkorps were linked.

In Poland the Germans experimented with so-called Air Signal Detachments. Two of them were given an armored car

---

*There is no exact USAF analogy to a fliegerkorps so it seems better to keep the German term. The fliegerkorps can be compared to the combat element of a tactical air force.

each, with radio, to accompany the commanders of supported armored division. "Greater use was made of these detachments in the French campaign, in which they proved indispensable." Here were TACP's in all but name.[8]

The French System Contrasted

French problems in air-ground cooperation began at the very top, in the mutual isolation of air and ground headquarters. Gen. Maurice Gamelin, Commander in Chief of the French Army worldwide, was at Vincennes, in the Paris urban area. His Chief of Air Staff, General Vuillemin, was at Coulommiers, 35 miles from Paris. General Georges, commanding the front from the Maginot Line to the sea, was 10 miles from Vuillemin, 40 from Gamelin. The air officer directly responsible for the northeast front, d'Astier de la Vigerie, was at Chaumy, 50 miles from Georges and even farther from Vuillemin.[9]

Each French army group was placed with a corresponding and subordinated Zone of Air Operations and requests for support from within the group had to go through army group headquarters, in contrast to the German corps/fliegerkorps link. These Zones of Air Operations had fighters allocated to them, and were under orders of the several army groups. Not only did this fritter away what fighter strength the French had but after a few days, in the developing crisis, contradictory orders were received through Armee de l'Air and army channels. The results were that on the critical day of 13 May, the French claimed but 21 German aircraft shot down in the Sedan area. On the 14th, of the 340 fighter sorties they put up, only 153 were over the area of the German breakthrough. They flew about 250 each on the 15th and 16th. On the latter day, these were scattered all the way from Antwerp to the Maginot Line. It may be remarked that these sorties were not close air support but the point here is not the nature of these sorties (which probably included fighter-bomber sorties) but the incoherence and disorganization of the French system of command and control in contrast to the precise application of German air power.[10]

The United States Begins to Adapt to Modern War

As is well known, the German conquests in Western Europe in April-June 1940 followed by the Battle of Britain caused great concern in Washington. In response, the United States mobilized its National Guard and Organized Reserves, began massive rearmament, expanded its air and naval power, and undertook to provide various forms of aid to the opponents of Germany, Italy, and Japan. War between the United States and Japan, then with Germany and Italy, began in December 1941. There followed a chain of events directly impacting on the evolution of U.S. air doctrine for command and control of close air support.

In December 1941, despite its expansion and demonstrated importance, the U.S. air arm was still organizationally a part of the U.S. Army. The Army's Chief of Staff, Gen. George C. Marshall, had reflected, however, on the lessons of World Wars I and II. At the Arcadia Conference (Washington, D.C., 22 December 1941-14 January 1942) of President Franklin D. Roosevelt, Prime Minister Winston S. Churchill, and their military advisers, Marshall carried his point that in theaters of operations there should be "unified command of combined forces," air, ground, and sea, by one officer. Next, the U.S. Joint Chiefs of Staff (JCS)--combining the Chief of Staff of the Army, the Chief of Naval Operations, and the head of the Army air, Gen. Henry H. Arnold, as colleagues--had their first meeting 9 February 1942. Then, on 9 March, the Army was reorganized into the Army Air Forces (AAF), the Army Ground Forces (AGF), and the Army Service Forces (ASF). However, only Arnold, head of the AAF, sat with the JCS. The heads of the AGF and ASF did not. In effect, the AAF was an independent service.

Consistent with these steps, Marshall radically reorganized the War Department General Staff by giving the Army Air Force about 50 percent of its posts. The former War Plans Division, renamed Operations Division (OPD), became a "central command post."11

The new Headquarters AAF set up a Directorate of Military Requirements which included Directorates of Group Support, Bombardment, and Air Defense. The Directorate of Ground Support inherited an almost complete draft field manual, based on the Louisiana and Carolina maneuvers of 1941. The draft was published 9 April 1942 as FM 31-35, <u>Aviation</u> <u>in</u> <u>Support</u> <u>of</u> <u>Ground</u> <u>Forces</u>.[12]

This edition of FM 31-35 was greatly concerned with organization and had little to say about employment of close air support. It provided that a theater of operations would have several Air Force commands, each of them "'habitually attached to or supports an army in the theater.'" This was reminiscent of the French Zone of Air Operations attached to an army group. Further, air units could be "'specifically allocated to the support of subordinate ground units.'" The air support commander was under the field army commander. As for employment and control, FM 31-35 stated that "'the most important target at a particular time will usually be that target which constitutes the most serious threat to the operations of the supported ground force. The final decision as to priority of targets rests with the commander of the supported unit.'" Also, "The decision as to whether or not an air support mission will be ordered rests with the commander of the supported unit. Such decision must comprehend full consideration of the air support commander's advisement (sic)..." As Air Force historians later pointed out, this was inconsistent with the doctrine then being so successfully employed by the British Eighth Army/RAF partnership in the Western Desert.[13]

Provisions of this edition of FM 31-35 which were to be in the mainstream of doctrine were that headquarters of the air support command and of the supported unit were collocated. "Air support parties" were allocated to division headquarters and below; "air support control" was preferably at corps, but might be at division. Requests originating with ground unit commanders went up through command channels until they reached a headquarters with an air support party. The latter advised the commander on technical aspects of the request. If he approved, the request went to air support control. Air support control officers in collaboration with the corps or division commander evaluated the request and provided data for an operational order; as noted above, the ground commander made the final decision.[14]

As a data base for deriving doctrine, the 1941 Louisiana and Carolina maneuvers drew authoritative contemporary criticism. It must be noted that they were an attempt to apply the lessons of the 1939-1940 German campaigns but it was humanly impossible for a large military organization to change overnight. On the credit side, the U.S. maneuvers included an emphasis on and growing capability in armored warfare and air-ground cooperation. Progress and adaptability were noted in the employment of the new triangular division, massed armor, and paratroops. However, comments of Army observers on air-ground cooperation procedures might have been made in 1918.[15]

In the critiques that followed the Carolina maneuvers, Arnold stated that air-ground cooperation had been largely ineffective. He said that despite the lessons of France and Poland, the ground forces had not made full use of "their air support."[16] Lt. Gen. Lesley J. McNair, who later became the commander of the Army Ground Forces, said that ground commanders had disregarded the air threat, as other observers had noted in Louisiana.[17]

Initially, the new Headquarters AAF was not ideally organized to deal with the doctrinal problems FM 31-35 and its data base foreshadowed. Arnold himself wanted to avoid being shielded from new ideas by his staff so he gave direct access to 31 officers, each of whom could sign papers for Arnold. This delegation resulted in a flow of miscellaneous publication, each with its fragment of AAF thought, going out to field commands. There were too many for the busy field commander and his staff to wade through and they did not give a clear coherent picture of "air doctrine and employment policies."

The system for solving the problem, once the experience and inputs were supplied, began to form with the reopening of the Tactical School. Its closing after the Japanese attack on Pearl Harbor, though defensible as a source for pilots in a time of national crisis, was soon recognized as shortsighted. The school reopened 27 October 1942 as the AAF School of Applied Tactics, Orlando, Fla. It used returned combat officers as instructors, which automatically provided the feedback of battle experience and practice. In line with past service practice, Headquarters AAF set up an AAF Board within the school to study the "'over-all picture of Air Force'" matters.[18] As combat experience accumulated, doctrine could be shaped accordingly.

Early Combat Experience in the Pacific
August-October 1942

Tactical air warfare in the Pacific began some months before the U.S. air-ground team closed with the Germans in North Africa. Beginning 22 August 1942, the 67th Fighter Squadron under the operational control of the 1st Marine Air Wing (1st MAW) gave close air support on Guadalcanal. In October, after the failure of ground panels a la World War I to link with contemporary aircraft, the Marines detailed an officer with radio equipment and operators to provide "'air forward observers'" for each regiment. This adaptation of contemporary U. S. Field Artillery terminology and practice was a pioneer effort,[19] and a first step toward the forward air controller (FAC). The term "air liaison officer" was applied in New Guinea in August-October 1942 to infantry or artillery officers who gave pre-mission briefings to pilots. The thick foliage made "...direct air support of the infantry especially difficult but useful experience in the employment of air liaison officers and smoke or signal panels was gained."[20]

The issue of interface between the services on problems relating to the control of tactical air had to be faced early in the Pacific. Though the aircraft involved initially were heavy bombers (B-17), their use was tactical. Headquarters, South Pacific Area (SPA) and U.S. Navy planners even as early as July 1942 had long been urging the deployment of B-17's. The problem lay in their command and control. The first solution was to appoint an air officer, Maj. Gen. Millard F. Harman, as commander of all Army forces (it will be recalled that these were the days of the Army Air Forces--USAAF not USAF). He was given a staff weighted toward air, and his headquarters with those of naval air were collocated with Headquarters SPA. Harmon initially told Arnold that SPA officers did not ask anything beyond his capabilities and that "'they freely consult unit commanders and members of my staff on matters of technique.'" The arrangement had been insisted on to insure that air units preserved their identity, received appropriate missions, and executed them under their own commanders in accordance with USAAF doctrine.[21]

However, it was Harmon's responsibility to see that Rear Admiral John R. McCain's operational control over the B-17's was exercised in accordance with USAAF doctrine. After some months he concluded that cooperation was not enough. A centralized, formal USAAF organization for the South Pacific Area was required and the Thirteenth Air Force was subsequently activated in January 1943.[22] By that date operations in North Africa were well under way and experience was demonstrating that the provisions of FM 31-35, which let ground commanders control their close air support, were seriously defective.

The Tunisian Lessons

As has been noted, the United States tried to modify its military doctrines and procedures to incorporate the lessons of 1939-1940 in the 2 years before it entered combat. Contact with the German Armed Forces was needed to show where and how far these modifications were defective. USAAF close air support in Tunisia initially was employed, commanded, and controlled in accord with FM 31-35. The U.S. Twelfth Air Force during November 1942-February 1943 had been divided into air support, air defense, bombardment, and air service commands. Its XII Air Support Command had been attached to the U.S. II Corps. It operated both fighter and bombardment squadrons.[23] II Corps had little interest in events outside its corps boundaries. Moreover, Allied all-weather fields were well to the rear, which was a severe operational handicap; the enemy's, on the other hand, were close to the front.[24]

Observing these arrangements, Air Marshal Sir Arthur Coningham, in addressing senior American and British officers in February 1943, said that the lessons of the Western Desert had been ignored in planning the North African operations.[25]

When Field Marshal Erwin Rommel took the initiative and attacked in February 1943, the command and control of American (and British) close air support--plus the siting of Allied air fields --contributed to the series of minor disasters and major setbacks that are grouped under the words, Kasserine Pass. Contemporary comment ran:[26]

> The air arm was unable either to protect Allied ground troops from dive bombing and strafing or to attack enemy ground troops holding up allied advances.

>...The minute those Spitfires went away, the German planes came right out and were on us again. One of our battalions was dive-bombed as many as 22 times in one day. (Intvw, Hqs AAF with Brig. Gen. Lunsford E. Oliver, 1st Armd Div, 5 Feb 43.)

>...nor could I find any case where ground troops had received close battle support from the air. (Comments, Maj. Gen. John P. Lucas, Eisenhower's American deputy, 1 Apr 43.)

One observer confused cause and effect:[27]

>In some cases, as at Faid Pass, the absence of observation and of close air support may have spelled the difference between disaster and success. So little close-in support was given that it did not offer an adequate test of existing procedures. (Rprt of Col. Henry V. Dexter, 11 Jun 43, subj: Air-Ground Support in North Africa; AGF and Air Ground Battle Team, Study No. 35, 17 Jul 48.)

Command and control was radically changed while the Kasserine Pass battle was still being fought. The month before, Churchill, Roosevelt, and their military advisers met at Casablanca and agreed on new command arrangements. These reflected the fact that the victorious Eighth Army/RAF team from the Western Desert had driven Rommel westward into Tunisia; the North African and Middle Eastern Allied commands had to be combined into one. The Kasserine debacle made the matter one of urgency. The result for Tunisia was this structure, in order of rank:

Name	Commander	Activation Date
Mediterranean Air Command	Air Chief Marshal Tedder	17 Feb 1943
Northwest African Air Forces	Maj. Gen. Spaatz	18 Feb 1943
Northwest African Tactical Air Force	Air Marshal Coningham	18 Feb 1943

Coningham's command included No. 242 Group, RAF; XII Air Support Command, and the Western Desert Air Force, RAF. His task was direct air support of the British and American ground forces facing the Italo-German bridgehead in Tunisia.[28]

The Air Force historians point out that these arrangements recognized[29]

> ...that the air forces cooperating with the ground battle had to be fought under a single air commander, since the planes, unlike the ground components, moved freely over the battlefield and could be employed in any part of it.

Under these arrangements, the official Army history later stated:

> Support of ground operations by Allied aviation during the last phase of the Tunisian campaign took the form of attack on enemy troops and positions in the path of ground attack with much greater frequency than it had earlier.

The issue of centralized control of direct air support by the tactical air force commander was seemingly settled in Tunisia. What remained to be done was to reconcile unified control of tactical air with the Army's demand that tactical air be able to meet immediate requests from subordinate Army units. The same Army history observes that the only remedy contemporaneously suggesting itself to the ground forces was operational control of allocated air by Army commanders,[30] which had been tried and rejected in Tunisia. The next tasks were to recast AAF doctrine for close air support in the light of the Tunisian experience and find a way to fill the immediate request.

Publishing a Charter for Tactical Air

In January 1943, General Sir Bernard L. Montgomery (as he then was) published his reflections on the conduct of war. They found a receptive audience in Marshall, Arnold and most of Arnold's air associates. Looking back on his cooperation, as ground force commander, with the RAF's Western Desert Air Force,

Montgomery asserted that the greatest asset of air power was its flexibility, which could only be realized when air was under the central control of an air officer working in close association with the ground commander:[31]

> Nothing could be more fatal to successful results than to dissipate the air resources into small packets placed under command of army formation commanders, with each packet working on its own plan.

Arnold and Brig. Gen. Laurence S. Kuter, his principal planner, wholeheartedly approved Montgomery's suggestion that air should be organized functionally into strategic and tactical air forces. They felt that this would free strategic air from having to meet "routine" ground force needs. Headquarters AAF asked the War Department to set up a board (which was done 9 June 1943) to revised Army/AAF doctrine in the light of recent experience. The result was FM 100-20, <u>Field Service Regulations, Command and Employment of Air Power,</u> 21 July 1943.

Using capital letters in the original to emphasize its basic message, FM 100-20 totalled only 14 pages. It laid down explicitly that land power and air power were coequal and interdependent: "neither is an auxiliary of the other." Following Montgomery, it said that the inherent flexibility of air power was its greatest asset. Its control must be centralized and command exercised through the air force commander. The theater commander

> ...will exercise command of air forces through the air force commander and command of ground forces through the ground force commander. The superior commander will not attach Army air forces to units of the ground force under his command except when such ground forces units are operating independently or are isolated by distance or lack of communication.

FM 100-20 provided that tactical air and ground force operations would be coordinated by timely planning conferences of commanders and staffs and through the exchange of liaison officers. "Air and ground liaison officers will be officers who are well versed in air and ground tactics." The strategic air force in "particularly opportune" situations might "be diverted to tactical air force missions."

The provisions in FM 100-20 for direct air support and its control indicated that a great deal of work had still to be done.[32]

> Massed air action on the immediate front will pave the way for an advance. However, in the zone of contact, missions against hostile units are most difficult to control, are most expensive, and are, in general, least effective. Targets are small, well-dispersed, and difficult to locate. In addition, there is always a considerable chance of striking friendly forces due to errors in target designation, errors in navigation or to the fluidity of the situation. Such missions must be against targets readily identified from the air, and must be controlled by phase lines, or bomb safety lines which are set up and rigidly adhered to by both ground and air units. Only at critical times are contact zone missions profitable.

There were real practical difficulties keeping Headquarters AAF and its agencies and commands in the Continental United States (CONUS) from making further advances in the field of doctrine in the 2 years that remained of World War II, i.e., June 1943-August 1945. First, it was hard to get qualified personnel. Then, masses of reports from the field had to be read and digested. Finally, it was extremely difficult, if not in practice impossible, to get Headquarters Army Ground Forces to concur. Thus, a draft training circular on air-ground cooperation did not get AGF concurrence in April 1944. Then, in January 1945, AGF attacked FM 100-20 itself. As a result, the several overseas theaters had to work out their own solutions to the remaining problems of the command and control of close air support.[33] In effect, formal doctrine was frozen well into 1945, but progress did not stand on formality.

The Theaters Find a Way to Control "Contact Zone Missions"

As noted above, FM 100-20's paragraph 16 had rather deprecated close air support. But the Army's demands for close air support were a real world problem known to the airmen who were now in close association with coequal Army staffs and commanders so ingenious airmen in the Pacific, the Mediterranean, and China-Burma-India theaters worked out solutions.

In the Pacific, we find that even before publication of FM 100-20--at some date between January and June 1943--air liaison officers are placed with supported units. In September 1943 the air liaison officers going ashore at Finschhafen, New Guinea, have enlisted subordinates, radio sets, and are called "detachment commanders." At Cape Gloucester, December 1943, the detachment is formally identified as the 1st Air Liaison Party. It is now a true tactical air control party, though not so named, for "It controlled bomber strikes by messages direct to the pilots."[34] Targets were marked by smoke shells or shell bursts, or strikes were requested by coordinates.[35]

In Italy, the Fifth Army and XII Tactical Air Command in 1944-1945 had collocated headquarters with nightly planning conferences. Immediate requests for close air support went from Army units at the front to the Army Air Section. The appropriate corps monitored them. Its silence was a positive indication that it approved a request it could not meet from its own resources. Army G-3 and XII TAC officers then decided if the mission should be flown. About 50 percent of immediate requests were refused. Of these, Army G-3 disapproved about 75 percent as not in line with its plans and TAC officers disapproved the balance on technical grounds. At the front, experienced pilots served tours guiding strike aircraft to their targets. When the mountainous terrain of Italy required, they operated from liaison aircraft.[36] In short, as they took to the air, they became the true forward air controllers that we know today.

The organization for tactical air control in the European Theater of Operations (ETO) was an expansion of that used in Italy. The Ninth Air Force cooperated closely with 12th Army Group, its subordinate commands with the several U. S. armies:

IX TAC ------------First Army

XIX TAC ------------Third Army

XXIX TAC ------------Ninth Army

The Ninth Air Force kept its medium bombers and tactical reconnaissance aircraft under its own headquarters' control. On occasion, these reconnaissance aircraft guided fighter-bombers to targets of opportunity.

The use of radar to control Ninth Air Force fighter-bombers
--particularly the excellent P-47--is a technological development
that must be underscored. It will be recalled that neither early-
warning nor control radars were present in France in 1940. But
in 1944, control and reporting centers and posts, under whatever
local name, kept the installations and agencies directing tactical
air instantaneously and continually aware of the air situation.

In static periods, about 10 percent of Ninth Air Force capability was allocated to close air support, the balance being armed
reconnaissance and interdiction. It routinely prepared to commit
15 percent of its capability to close air support. On occasion, all
air capabilities would be massed for close air support. Thus, as
will be discussed in detail below, 1,500 heavy bombers on 25 July
1944 prepared the way for the U.S. First Army to break out of
the Normandy beachhead.[37]

USAAF tactical air control system in Burma, May 1944, is
particularly significant as illustrating its original solution to the
operational and geographic problems of controlling close air support in Southeast Asia. It involved:[38]

> ...a technique for air support in siege [i.e., Myitkyina]
> or mobile warfare. For the former, A-2 and A-3 were
> responsible for joint planning with the task force G-2
> and G-3. The latter two chose the targets, while the
> air staff "planned the attack, determined the type and
> number of aircraft to be used, the types of bombs, the
> techniques of attack, the selection of the units...and
> the briefing of the crews."

For mobile warfare there was the "air party." This was a team
of one or 2 officers with 6 to 8 enlisted men, who were linked by
air to the "air office." Located at brigade or regimental headquarters, they gave "immediate information on targets selected by
the army and approved by the air party. They also served as
guides to aircraft which were making air strikes." If their position did not permit them to observe the tactical situation, "an
L-5 was used for strike observation, which worked through the
air party.... In some cases aircraft were over the target thirty
minutes after the original request."

Therefore, early in 1944 the elements of the tactical air control system as it is known today, from the forward air controller up to the air operations center, had been developed. They were being applied in the jungles of Burma and the mountains of Italy, and partly so in the hedgerows of Normandy. A particularly impressive demonstration of close air support was given in Normandy 25 July 1944.

Close Air Support Prepares the Normandy Breakout

After the Allies had successfully crossed the Channel 6 June 1944 and established a firm bridgehead in Normandy, the Germans succeeded in confining them to that part of France. Repeated Allied attacks, by ground and air, steadily wore down German strength. Montgomery tried to break out with his British and Canadian troops on 18 July, after some 1,000 heavies and 350 mediums dropped 7,700 tons of bombs on the German defenses in their path, but Operation Goodwood failed. The reasons for the failure involved the ground forces,* this was seen, and American commanders were anxious to repeat the air preparation.[39]

Gen. Omar N. Bradley, commanding the U.S. First Army, presented his requirements in person to the senior air officers concerned. He wanted them to bomb an area of about 6 square miles. In classic fashion, his infantry would attack immediately thereafter to take maximum advantage of the preparation. He also indicated the type of ordnance he wanted, to avoid excessive cratering (which also had bedeviled the British in Goodwood). The airmen replied that they could deliver blast effect by a mass attack, they could use bombs that would minimize cratering, and could attack the desired target area. They could not get the desired mass if they used the approach parallel to the front that Bradley suggested for safety, and also thought his proposed

---

*Among other mishaps, a good part of the forces that were to attempt the breakout were snarled in a monumental traffic jam. Meanwhile, the Germans put a screen of their ubiquitous and effective 88-mm. all-purpose guns across the gap opened by the air bombardment.

800-yard safety zone too small. Bradley finally agreed to a somewhat wider safety zone that would be narrowed by fighter-bombers after the heavies were finished. The attack would have the combined resources of the Eighth and Ninth Air Forces.

Illustrating the state of the control art in the ETO July 1944, there was no direct radio link air-to-ground so visual means would be used. The infantry were to move forward as soon as the heavies had finished and while the fighter-bombers were narrowing the safety zone. The infantry was to reach the line of departure when the fighter-bombers finished; their rate of advance was set accordingly. Unhappily, a partly cancelled bombing on the originally planned day, the 24th, showed in its execution that there had been no clear understanding as to the line of approach. Human error resulted in killing 25 and wounding 131 American troops. The conference had not, after all, been enough.[40]

The bombing as originally planned was executed on the 25th. About 1,500 heavies, 380 mediums, and 559 fighter-bombers dropped 4,200 tons of bombs on about 6 square miles. Again, a bombardier's error led 77 bombers to unload over American positions, killing 111 (among them General McNair, commanding AGF) and wounding 490. But the shadow of this tragedy could not conceal the success of the bombing and the success of the American infantry exploiting. At the end of the first day, though the officers and men of the attacking units did not know it, U.S. VII Corps had broken through the defenses hastily improvised by those Germans who had survived the bombing.

About one-third of the Germans on the main line of resistance and in immediate reserve were killed or wounded by the AAF. The rest were dazed. "The bombardment transformed the main line of resistance from a familiar pastoral paysage into a frightening landscape of the moon."

Considering the sporadic nature of the German resistance on the 25th, that night the corps commander, Maj. Gen. Lawton J. Collins, decided that certain key roads were sufficiently uncovered for him to commit his armor. That decision made, all else followed, for the air and infantry had broken the only organized German defenses between Normandy and the German border.[41]

ETO practice as regards forward air control began to pull abreast of Fifth Army/XII TAC when on 20 July, just before the breakout, Maj. Gen. Elwood Quesada, commanding IX TAC, suggested that an Air Support Party (ASP) be put in each of the 4 combat commands of the 2 armored divisions that were to exploit the breakthrough. Each ASP was to have an AAF-type VHF radio. This would permit 2-way links between the columns and the 4-ship flights that were to provide close armed reconnaissance for the combat commands. The ground commanders would monitor the fighter-bombers channel C to receive information. They could also request the flights to attack targets. Targets which IX TAC could not handle would go back through ASP channels and be attacked by fighter-bombers on strip alert. The flights overhead were also in touch with their home controller and would at once report anything of interest to him.

Such a report followed the discovery of a German column blocked on the east by the U.S. 2d Armored Division and on the west by elements of the 3d. It was worked over for 6 hours by relays from the 405th Fighter-Bomber Group. When U.S. troops reached the spot, they found 121 destroyed or damaged German tanks. This may be compared with the panzer division's authorized tank strength of 176, a happy state rarely found in the German Army in summer 1944.[42]

By August 1944, forward air controllers in L-5 aircraft--so-called "horseflys"--were guiding "fighter-bombers to targets selected by ground" in France.[43] That General Quesada, the IX TAC commander, had found the same solution to the problem of cooperation between air and armor that the Germans had found 5 years before strongly suggests--as do the other parallels between German and American practice--that the principles of command and control of close air support are independent of nationality, even as the parallels between practice in Italy, France, and Burma suggest they are independent of geography.

Thus, by 1945 AAF practice of the command and control of close air support had reached a very high degree of sophistication and combat effectiveness. In about 12 months, airmen had gone far beyond FM 100-20 and the time had come to transform their practices to doctrine.

The Lessons of World War II: FM 31-35

Because it was necessary in early 1945 to begin preparations for the invasion of Japan, the Operations Division of the War Department put an end to the tacit doctrinal freeze that ensued on the appearance of FM 100-20. Itself at the highest level in the War Department, manned by Army and AAF officers, it could direct both AAF and AGF; the compromises reached in OPD were binding on both and may well have resulted from negotiations now lost in the passage of 26 years. This permitted issuance of Training Circular No. 17, Air-Ground Liaison, on 20 April and No. 30, Tactical Air Command: Organization and Employment, 19 June.

With the doctrinal freeze broken, the end of the war in August 1945 gave the occasion to produce doctrinal publications incorporating the lessons of World War II. To this end, Headquarters AAF 7 September 1945 directed the AAF Board to proceed accordingly. A month later it directed revision of FM 100-20. The first publication to result was a manuscript on air-ground operations. Headquarters AGF concurred, the War Department approved, and its 75 printed pages appeared 13 August 1946 as FM 31-35, <u>Air-Ground Operations</u>. In the later opinion of the Air Force historian, Dr. Robert Frank Futrell, both Army and AAF officers were so pleased with the system used in ETO that they wrote it up as FM 31-35.[44]

An examination of Figures 1-4 from FM 31-35 (reproduced on pp 22, 23, 24) shows that the manual was a re-affirmation and expansion of FM 100-20 of 1943 to which was added the result of combat experience in the command and control of close air support. Figures 1 and 2 show the basic command relationships resulting from experience in North Africa and the Western Desert. Figure 3 shows the expansion and formalization of FM 100-20's terse statement that tactical air and ground force operations would be coordination by timely planning conferences and exchanging liaison officers. Now there is a system with its own nomenclature and subsystems.

The new tactical air control system described in FM 31-35 represented progress beyond the point at which, it will be recalled, FM 100-20 stopped. Chapter 5, with 23 pages, tells how to organize, operate, and administer the system. According to FM 31-35:

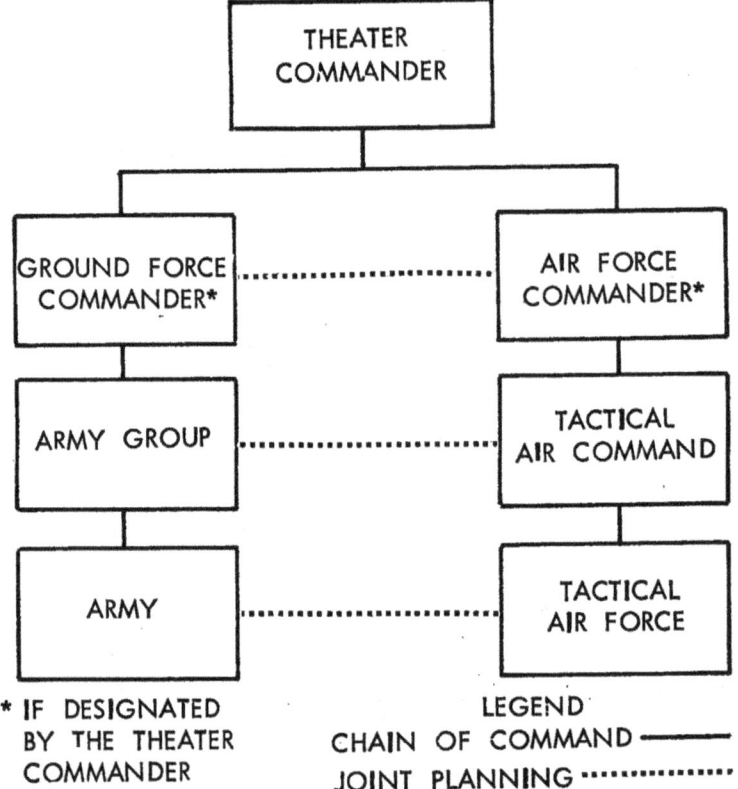

Figure 1

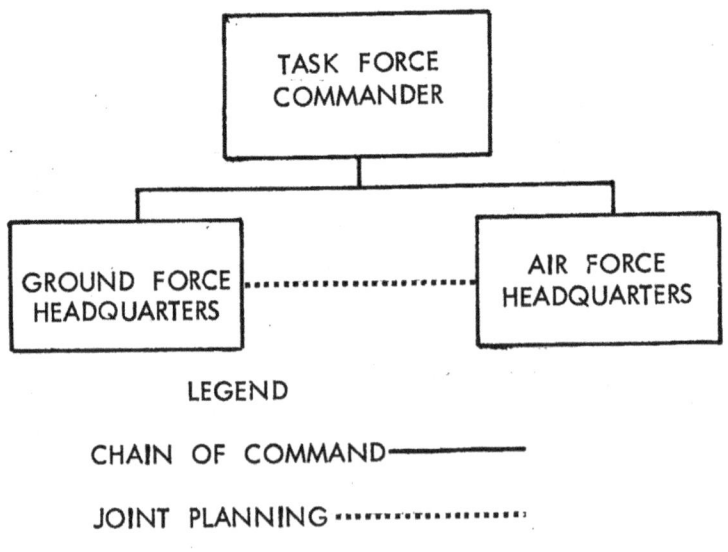

Figure 2

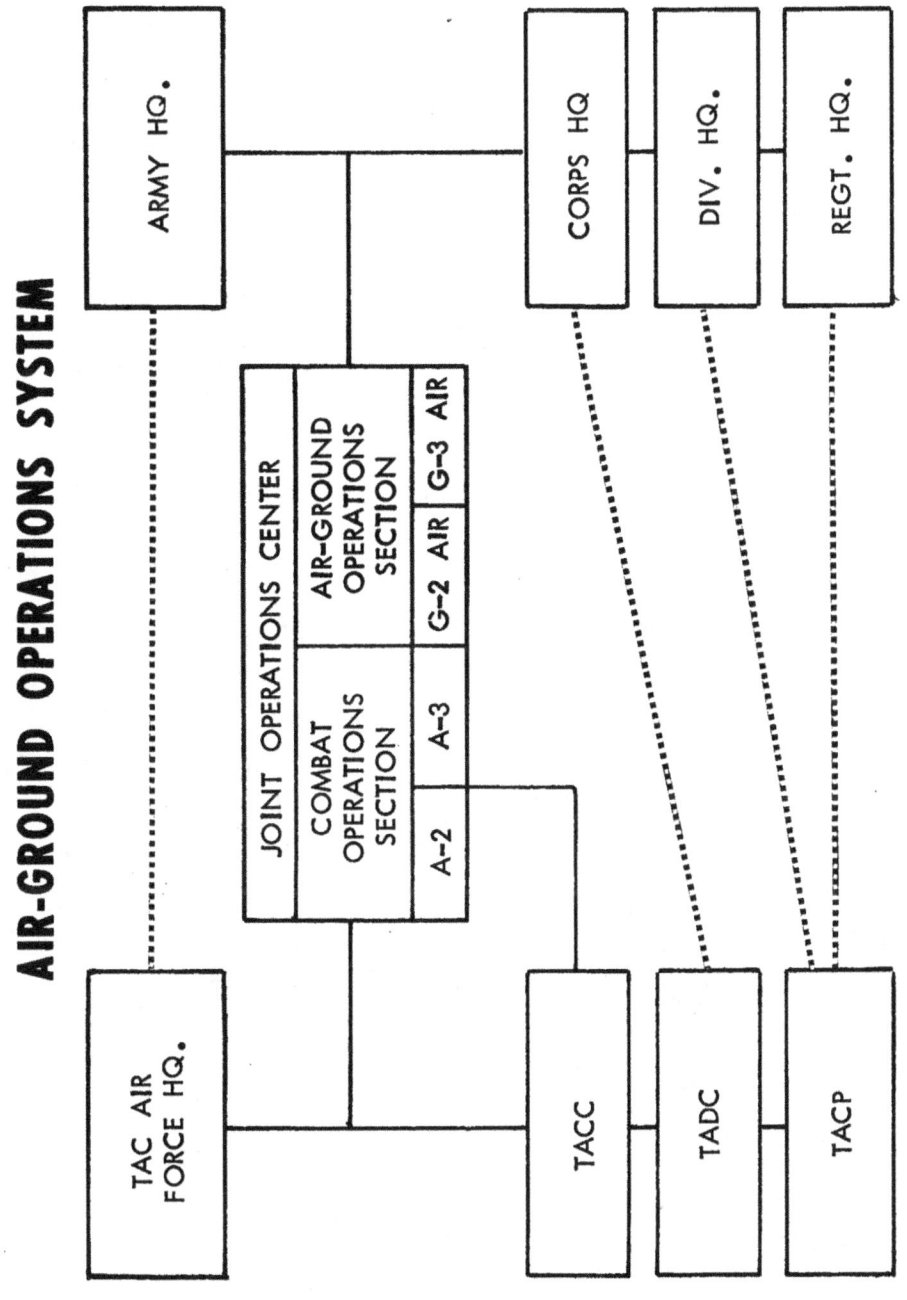

Figure 3

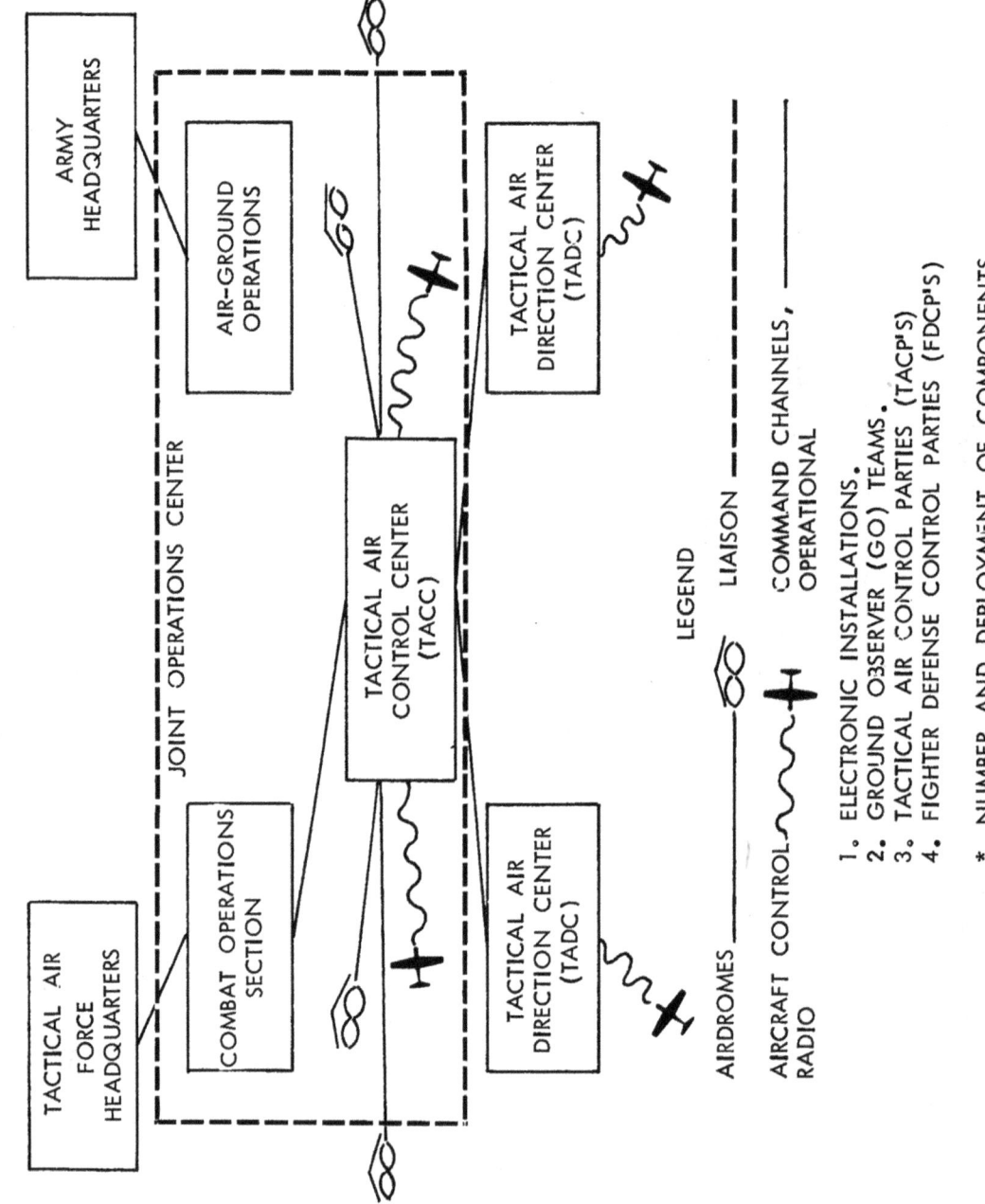

Figure 4

The tactical air control center (TACC) is the focal point for the tactical air force's control and warning activity. It should be located with or near the TAF combat operations section.

The tactical air direction center (TADC) is a subordinate air control installation directing aircraft and air warning operations in a restricted area. Its scale may be large or small.

The tactical air control party is a forward air controller with assistants as needed who operate under a TACC or TADC. FAC operations are described in familiar terms.

The air liaison officer did not receive his acronym of ALO, was not a part of the air-ground operation system, could not seek air support but did "assist in advising on normal air requests processed through ground channels."

An issue of considerable importance was placed rather near the end of the manual. Paragraph 55 b (6) provided that the Army would transmit requests for air support.

The Doctrinal Background to Korea: TACS

FM 31-35 was to have been part of a major effort at producing up-to-date doctrinal publications. This intent was nullified by the scarcity of qualified personnel in the immediate postwar period. The further question of where in what was now the U.S. Air Force doctrine would be produced was not easy to answer. The initial solution was to give the new Air University the task. Indeed, Maj. Gen. Lauris Norstad argued that the concentration of the Air Force's ablest officers at the Air University as instructors and students would result in the production of "'usable doctrine'" even if they were not formally tasked with the mission. So the Air University was directed to develop basic doctrines and concepts for employment of air power, publish them, do related research, and involve itself in testing. However, this involved adjustments with the field commands, some of which also had doctrinal responsibilities.[45]

In his last report as Chief of Staff of the Air Force, Gen. Carl Spaatz suggested in mid-1948 that the mission of the Tactical Air Command required it to develop and test related doctrines and techniques. Notably, TAC's headquarters had been put at Langley Field, Va., a short drive from Fort Monroe, site of Headquarters Army Field Forces. The intent of the collocation had been close daily contact between the personnel of the 2 headquarters, an application of FM 100-20 and FM 31-35. However, this arrangement and General Spaatz' suggestion were moves away from the Air University role.

In February 1949, TAC's Deputy for Plans was working with representatives of Army Field Forces (AFF) to draft a joint paper for an Ad Hoc JCS Committee for Joint Policies and Procedures. The purpose was to define areas of agreement and disagreement on the tactical air support of ground forces. These Army personnel soon indicated to TAC that their headquarters no longer concurred in the air-ground organization envisaged by FM 31-35. This was believed by the airmen to reflect Army dissatisfaction with the current organizational stature of TAC, which was then a part of the Continental Air Command. This latter command was much more nearly equal to AFF's place in the Army organization.[46]

Although the TAC/AFF representatives could not agree on a draft, their superiors proceeded with plans to set up a Hqs Tactical Air Force (Provisional) at Pope AFB which would work with Hqs V Corps nearby at Fort Bragg to plan and conduct joint maneuvers. With this development, work on a second draft by the TAC/AFF working party went more smoothly, so that a draft joint training directive (JTD) had most of its chapters by March 1950. If approved, it would then be tested by the TAF/V Corps set-up. As written, the directive was an amplification of the principles and revision of the means and procedures of FM 31-35.

However, the beginning of the Korean War in June 1950 obliged the cancellation of most tests and maneuvers, yet made the need for such a training directive even more urgent. Because of this urgency, the Vice Commander of TAC, Brig. Gen. Homer L. Sanders, and AFF's Chief of Staff, Brig. Gen. William S. Lawton, published the directive 1 September 1950. Under its charter, AFF could issue the directive as doctrine for Army training in the Zone of the Interior, which it commanded. For its part, TAC could only hope that other Air Force commands would accept the documents.

The Air University strongly criticized some parts on the grounds that they departed from FM 31-35. However, its criticisms addressed the directive's treatment of tactical air forces. The Air University would have preferred a line of thought dealing with the tactical uses of air forces, i.e., theater air forces rather than tactical air forces. These criticisms did not touch the theme of this study, the evolution of CAS command and control. There, as Korean practice soon showed, the directive was squarely in the mainstream. These Air University views did not prevent final Air Force approval of the JTD on 9 March 1951 so that there might be "uniformity in all air-ground training and instruction throughout the Air Force."[47] While these discussions were proceeding, fighting in Korea had been heavy and at times desperate, subjecting the Air Force's doctrine of command and control of close air support to its severest test since 1944.

Korea Confirms FM 31-35 on TACS

The tactical air control system laid down by FM 31-35 and amplified by the JTD of 1 September 1950 was used throughout the Korean conflict, June 1950-July 1953. Fifth Air Force established a joint operations center, sent TACP's all the way down to regiment, and found the men and equipment for an Eighth Army air request net pending arrival from the CONUS of Army signal assets. When Japan-based jets could not remain over the lines long enough to identify their targets, the provisions of FM 31-35's paragraph 45 a--"Some situations favor the employment of a tactical air coordinator for assisting and directing the attacking aircraft"-- were applied. Fifth Air Force provided them in Mosquito T-6's to identify targets and control attacks. When the 1st Marine Air Wing ended independent operations in December 1950, it was deployed to South Korea and came under a Joint Operations Center (JOC). It was then possible to mass all assets, Far East Air Forces Bomber Command, Fifth Air Force, Seventh Fleet carrier aviation, and 1st MAW, for close air support.[48]

Though this unified control included the Marines and the Navy, the JOC's practice acknowledged the realities of the situation. Marine air was in great part a compensation for the small Marine component of organic field artillery in situations of prolonged commitment outside the range of naval guns as in Korea. Consequently, Marine Corps senior officers were alert to any possibility of losing their own close air support. Meanwhile, use of carrier aviation added its problems of communications and protocol.

Recognizing that the 1st MAW had the command capabilities of a task force, Fifth Air Force gave it "considerable latitude for planning and ordering its air operations." Orders almost always went through its commander. The only bypassing was immediate requests for close air support via hot-line telephone to Marine pilots on strip alert. In turn, Marine liaison officers gave Fifth Air Force morning planning conferees a report on their unit's intentions and capabilities.

Carrier air from Task Force (TF) 77 did not fit in quite so easily. Beginning November 1950 and continually thereafter the Seventh Fleet maintained continuous-wave and very high frequency (VHF) voice radio links with the JOC. Daily by 1200, Seventh Fleet would give the JOC its schedule for the following day. The JOC would then ask assignment of aircraft to various missions. Unhappily, the radio links were often uncertain so that the exact status of carrier air would then become equally uncertain while the U.S. Navy liaison officer at the JOC could not order sorties but only relay the JOC's requests. The result was close air support by carrier air that was valuable but not easily integrated.[49]

The First Days in Korea: CAS without TACS

In the opening phases of the Korean War the enemy enjoyed the advantages of tactical and strategic surprise and complete combat readiness. The American and South Korean governments had to appraise the situation, their armed forces had to react and improvise while events steadily outran the steps earlier thought adequate to meet them.

The North Korean People's Army attacked on Sunday 25 June 1950. That afternoon President Syngman Rhee pled for U.S. air cover for his army. This began a process of escalating the role of U.S. air which is largely beyond the scope of this paper. However, very late on the 26th (Washington time) President Harry S. Truman approved the suggestion of Secretary of State Dean G. Acheson that the U.S. Navy and U.S. Air Force support and cover the Republic of Korea (ROK) forces <u>below</u> the 38th parallel. This confined the Air Force for the moment to the close-in tactical role.

During the night of the 27th (local time), Far East Air Forces (FEAF) was directed to attack "tanks, artillery, and military columns, supply dumps, ground transport, bridges, and moving traffic..." No contingency plans for this existed. Meanwhile, at the front the ROK troops were under such pressure that their commander thought that day he had lost 40 percent of his effectives and was not sure of the location of his units. How, under these circumstances, was close air support to be directed? How soon could a TACS be set up?

Though weather offered problems, interdiction and armed reconnaissance began on the 28th. That same day, two TACP's were dispatched to Korea with the hope they could work with ROK troops while Lt. Col. John McGinn, USAF, at the advanced echelon (ADCOM) of Far East Command, Suwon, by authority of expediency began to act as a one-man TACS. He picked likely targets in front of what he was told the ROK front line, then radioed them to fighters orbiting above. The TACP's reached Suwon, could not be deployed, and stayed with ADCOM. Over the 29th and 30th McGinn kept on. "Working as he was, almost single-handed, Colonel McGinn could not provide many close support targets." On the 29th, FEAF appreciated the need for a full-fledged TACS and ordered Fifth Air Force to set up a tactical air direction center. But time was running out and next day ADCOM began a forced retreat to Taejon.

On the 30th (local time) a major restriction on the use of air power was lifted when the JCS authorized FEAF to work above the 38th parallel. The decision to commit ground troops followed and on 1 July the first planeloads of U.S. infantry arrived at Pusan. This must be measured against the fact that in the first week of combat the ROK army lost 44,000 men dead, captured, or missing, and with them 70 percent of its individual weapons.[50] In retrospect, one may wonder at the hopes attached to commitment of tactical air in the absence of a TACS, and the concomitant decision not to strike massively and at once at North Korean lines of communication, military installations, and troop concentrations.

With the commitment of U.S. troops came the opening of the air component of a joint operations center at 24th Division headquarters 5 July and the arrival of TACP's. Unhappily, this was not yet a fully effective TACS. The TACP's were in jeeps, not tanks or aircraft. They drew fire, and were completely vulnerable to the infiltrators and roadblocks so much a part of those grim days. Though the infantry were supposed to request fire on specific targets, they were all too often out of contact and could not do so. Trying to gather information, the ardent young tactical air controllers were often acting as jeep patrols, a role in which they were soft targets. The airborne FAC was the answer and 9 July they began to work, initially using the L-5G with 4-channel VHF radios.[51]

The problem of close air support for ROK troops was exacerbated by the language problem and there were cases of their being attacked in error. The interim solution was command insistence on a realistic bomb line and painting white stars on ROK vehicles.[52]

With establishment of the TACS in South Korea, and with its organization and functions following FM 31-35, the question became what the Army's commanders thought of the close air support they then received. During the first 3 days of September 1950 when the North Korean Peoples Army was conducting its Naktong River offensive against the Pusan perimeter, the Fifth Air Force added its weight to that of the U.S. divisions' artillery for close support. Maj. Gen. William R. Kean, commanding the 25th Infantry Division, remarked at the time: "'The close air support rendered by Fifth Air Force again saved this division as they have many times before.'" Summing up his reaction to the events of summer and early fall 1950, Lt. Gen. Walton H. Walker, Eighth Army commander, said in November 1950: "'I will gladly lay my cards right on the table and state that if it had not been for the air support we received from the Fifth Air Force we would not have been able to stay in Korea.'"[53]

Weighing the Korean Experience

As noted above, the provisions of FM 31-35 as regards TACS applied throughout the Korean war with one exception ordered in the last month of the conflict. On 2 July 1953 the Air Force and Army agreed that henceforth the latter would provide both equipment and enlisted men for TACP's. The Air Force would continue to supply the airborne coordinator. However, adherence to FM 31-35 did not mean that the Army and Air Force had the same reading of the lessons of Korea. As early as the winter 1950-1951, the Army was arguing that field army and in some cases corps should have operational control of close air support units giving them reconnaissance and fire support. Gen. Lawton J. Collins, Chief of Staff, and General Mark Clark, Chief of Army Field Forces, so maintained. They envisaged specially made close support aircraft. (One may surmise that Marine Corps concepts of the organization and control of close air support, seen at first hand in Korea though in a permissive air environment, had not gone unnoticed.) Interservice conferences, service journals, all entered this discussion of roles and missions, command and control.

When General Clark as Commander in Chief, Far East, was later given a proposal to attach a squadron of Marine air to each of Eighth Army's 3 corps, he effectively reversed himself, pointing out that World War II (which he had seen from responsible rank in Italy) had shown the unwisdom of breaking air into penny packets, while giving each Army division air on the Marine scale would be impossibly expensive.[54]

At the end of the Korean war, representatives of all the services met in Seoul to discuss joint air-ground operations. They endorsed the system as used in Korea, as modified in its last month, and asked for "a joint air-ground doctrine that would encompass all services."[55]

Reaching agreement on joint air-ground doctrine in the early 1950's proved very difficult. Though the JCS set up a series of joint boards, including one on tactical air support, they proved sterile, and on 3 December 1954 the JCS ordered them dissolved. During these years, the U.S. Army was beginning to see potentialities in the helicopter that had not earlier been apparent, and these may have made it reluctant to enter into binding discussions. In Harpers magazine, April 1954, Maj. Gen. James H. Gavin offered the sky cavalry concept. There would be helicopter-borne troops that would execute the classic cavalry missions. In so doing they would expend ordnance.[56] Meanwhile, the Air University, as General Norstad had foreseen and its role required, had continued its keen interest in doctrine. It had worked away at formulating basic air doctrine as the foundation for all other. When in March 1953 the Air Council approved AFM 1-2, the basic manual, its action cleared the way to proceed with derivative topics, of which one was theater air forces. The administrative device used was a broad-based conference, drawn from the major air force commands, which considered draft manuals on counter-air, interdiction, and close air support.

The conferees opted for one manual combining all three and with representatives of the major commands gathered together, coordination was easy. The result was AFM 1-7, _Theater Air Forces in Counter Air, Interdiction, and Close Air Support Operations,_ 1 March 1954.[57] Obviously, it was air doctrine, not joint, as far as its legal status went.

In all of AFM 1-7's provisions as regards the Tactical Air Control System, there can be found only one shift from FM 31-35's language and one innovation. Where FM 31-35 called the joint operations center a "combined activity," AFM 1-7 stressed that it was an Air Force facility--the combat operations room of the tactical air force--in which there would be ground force representatives. Later experience in Vietnam would indicate this had significance. The innovation was the target director post, an attempt to use radar for control of air strikes. This in turn reflected the problem of directing strikes in Korea's mountains during night (a favored time for enemy attacks) or bad weather.[58]

Doctrinal Trends on the Eve of Vietnam

In the late 1950's the Army's growing interest in using helicopters and adding to its organic aviation suggested that pressures were building which would affect the TACS, and even introduce the problem of controlling the air space over the battlefield. In January 1955 Gen. Matthew B. Ridgway, then the Army's Chief of Staff, said that the Joint Training Directive used in the Korean War contained views on command responsibilities and service relationships which the Department of the Army could no longer accept in regard to air-ground operations. A year later, Maj. Gen. Hamilton Howze suggested that Army helicopter units should be given the capability to undertake pursuit and exploitation missions as well as reconnaissance and security.[59]

The Army, meanwhile, was testing an aerial reconnaissance and security troop. It included 16 observation and 11 larger helicopters, some with rockets and machine guns. One may note that in 1944 rocket-armed Hawker Typhoon fighters excelled as close support ground-attack fighters, carrying eight 3-inch rockets, disappointing though they had been as standard day fighters. Now, Army helicopters were acquiring the firepower of a fighter of, say, 11 years before. In speed, range, and armament, helicopters were moving along a curve which promised in the foreseeable future to bring them at least up to the level of combat aircraft of the late 1930's.[60]

In adjusting doctrinal differences between the Air Force and the Army as regarded close air support, interface was provided by the TAC/AFF and later TAC/Continental Army Command (CONARC) relationship. Field activities, though, as with the Army's at its Special Warfare Center at Fort Bragg and the Air Force's Special Air Warfare Center at Eglin, were not collocated. Establishment of the U.S. Strike Command might change the interface situation, for Secretary of Defense Robert S. McNamara in June 1962 said specifically that Strike Command's authorization to develop joint doctrine for the forces assigned to it would include the use of tactical air in coordination with ground forces, i.e., close air support.[61]

On the eve of Vietnam, the closest approach to joint doctrine was the successor to the Joint Training Directive of September 1950. As was its predecessor, it was issued jointly by TAC and CONARC. It bore the caveat that it did "not necessarily reflect approved doctrinal positions established by..." the Army, Navy, or Air Force. It sought to establish jointly acceptable operational procedures. Its provisions would govern TAC and CONARC training. This training would in turn largely determine what airmen and soldiers both would do in combat. The document was TACM 55-3/CONARC TT 110-100-1, Joint Air Ground Operations (JAGOS), 1 September 1957.

When JAGOS was being written, the Army was interested in the Pentomic concept for organization of its divisions. It called for helicopter-borne self-contained combat teams, which would disperse to survive nuclear attack, then assemble to fight. Their command and control would be facilitated by electronic data processing, computer net works linked to display devices, then new technological developments. Army tactical support centers with electronic displays, quantities of Army aviation, were very much present in CONARC's thinking and that of the Command and General Staff College (C&GSC), Fort Leavenworth, Kansas. The latter, indeed, had created the Pentomic concept.*
These ideas, in turn, are clearly reflected in JAGOS.

A major departure from FM 31-35 was the demise of the JOC. The ground force element was broken out and became a tactical support center (TSC). This, in turn, was the highest echelon in the chain of tactical support coordinating agencies at corps and division. No longer are they explicitly collocated or under the same roof with the air operating center. Thus, at field army the TSC is "in the same general location" and "maintains very close relations." Moreover, as the name suggests, the TSC and its subordinated agencies coordinated all tactical support available to their headquarters. This was army aviation, missiles, field artillery. They included G-2 and G-3 air personnel.

As the above paragraph implies, army organic aviation was given its own control system by JAGOS. The TSC had a direct support aviation center. This received and processed requests for air support. JAGOS explicitly stated that "Army requirements for close air and reconnaissance support are referred to the ASOC." However, directly under the direct support aviation center JAGOS placed a Flight Operations Center to control organic army aviation.

---

*From December 1955 to May 1958, the author of this study was in the Combat Operations Research Group, Headquarters CONARC, Fort Monroe, Va. He also visited the C&GSC, where Maj. Gen. Lionel C. McGarr was commandant. McGarr later took over the Military Advisory Group, Vietnam (MAAG-V).

The air component of the JOC became an air operations center (AOC), to assist the tactical air force commander within his area of responsibility. Tactical air force headquarters would also provide a highly mobile air support operations center (ASOC) for each field army headquarters. But the tactical air force now had air-ground responsibilities at army group level, which were to be discharged by exchange of liaison officers and normal staff contacts. The broadened role of this Army tactical air force reflected the disappearance of the World War II-type tactical air command.

Immediate requests would move up the chain battalion-division-TSC with corps monitoring. Each FAC would be supported by an Army-provided Air Control Team. ALO's and FAC's were under the ASOC.

As will be noted below, JAGOS' nomenclature and provisions, though they may not have been joint doctrine, were later used in Vietnam.

II. SOUTH VIETNAM, 1962-1969

TACS operations in South Vietnam spanned and were shaped by events in Southeast Asia (SEA) in two different periods. During 1961-1964 the United States sought to handle the situation by applying techniques of counterinsurgency and avoiding a commitment of large U.S. Army units. In 1965 it was obliged to deploy a number of Army and Marine Corps divisions which, in turn, required close air support on a massive scale. The Tactical Air Control System reflected this changing environment. In so doing, it displayed great flexibility.

The political and military environment of South Vietnam, 1961 through 1964, must be kept in mind. President Ngo Dinh Diem, who led the country until his overthrow in 1963, faced a situation in which the military and political were closely mingled. Consequently, as will be noted, very few officers of the Army of the Republic of Vietnam (ARVN) could approve air strikes and these, in turn, had to weigh the political consequences. And since this was an insurgency in which the guerrillas would attack populated places, requests for close air support would necessarily come from civil as well as the military authorities, implying a second and, at least partially, parallel air request net.

Further, the Air Force faced a situation fundamentally different from those of World War II and Korea. In Korea, there was no period of counterinsurgency. Divisions were committed as quickly as they could be provided. In World War II the AAF associated with the highly-qualified British armed forces when it operated in combined headquarters. In South Vietnam, the local lack of professional qualifications was the major part of the rationale for the U.S. presence. The Air Force had both to train and operate, and to train personnel from a very different culture with different personal situations and motivations. The operation of the TACS reflected this.

Setting Up the TACS in South Vietnam

When in January 1962 the Air Force began to advise and assist the Vietnamese Air Force (VNAF) in setting up a Tactical Air Control System, it found the local, formal command situation to be this:

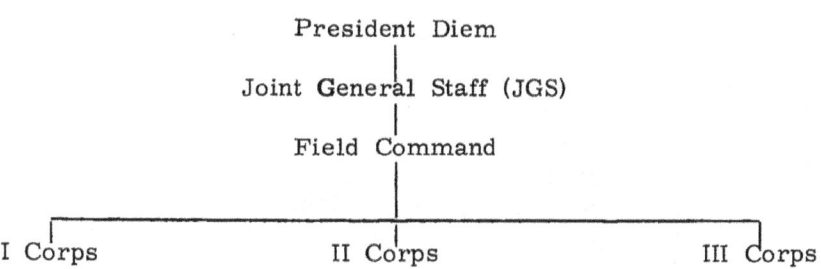

Both JGS and Field Command had to approve requests for air strikes, which did not improve the handling of immediate requests.[1] In collaboration with the Republic of Vietnam's armed forces, the Air Force proceeded to set up the familiar TACS system of jointly manned agencies. There was a Joint Operations Center with representatives of the Field Command and III Corps, and an AOC with a Vietnamese Director and USAF Deputy. The AOC and control and reporting center (CRC) were collocated at Tan Son Nhut. As VNAF personnel became available, ASOC's were opened, collocated with corps headquarters. The shortage of qualified VNAF personnel, which reflected an important reason for the USAF presence, required the deployment of USAF ALO's and the introduction of a small USAF FAC party. Initially, in line with doctrine, ALO's and FAC's were to have been attached to units. Soon it became apparent that VNAF FAC's were despatched, usually unbriefed, to supported units on an ad hoc basis, while the facts of counterinsurgency made sector and province headquarters as important as battalion and brigade or regiment in conventional war. Finally, this was sorted out. FAC's and ALO's went to area headquarters as well as field units and regular briefing of VNAF FAC's became standing operating procedure (SOP) in 1964.[2]

The TACS was to control both the VNAF and the small USAF elements initially committed to South Vietnam. From the beginning, the Army did not in practice permit it to control the

Army organic aviation that began appearing in South Vietnam, a development which had been foreshadowed by JAGOS, as noted above.*

The facts of Vietnam soon began to affect this setup. In the highest echelon, the JOC, the Vietnamese did not provide qualified officers. Their representatives were junior officers, uninformed, who simply relayed information to their superiors, and this over insecure communications. Finally, the JOC as known in doctrine simply atrophied and vanished. The absence of qualified Vietnamese ground officers--and it will be recalled that major U.S. ground units did not appear until 1965--also applied to the AOC and the ASOC's and drew comment from the JCS and Commander in Chief, Pacific (CINCPAC). The remedy was that Air Force ALO's and FAC's would advise the Vietnamese on the proper use of air and provide this form of air-ground interface.[3]

The U.S. Army's requirement that it control the air request net led in South Vietnam, 1962-1964, to ARVN operation of the net. The Vietnamese handled air support requests from ground force units as well as sector/district/province authorities' requests received from hamlets or villages and their paramilitary defenders. The power to refuse and the failure to transmit were built into this system.[4] The consequences and remedies will be discussed below.

The Problem of the Immediate Air Request Net

As the months went by in Vietnam, it became apparent that current doctrinal assignment of responsibility for the air request net to the ground forces, both for immediate and preplanned requests, was not producing satisfactory results. At the level of administrative and logistical support, U.S. Air Force FAC's and

---

*For example, in a message to higher headquarters, 2d Air Division stated: "We recognize that what follows is understood by the Air Staff...a JOC [sic] controlling only a portion of the total air effort... ." [See Msg 20DC-62-1994J (S), 2d AD AFSSO to CSAF and PACAF, 30 Oct 62.]

ALO's found that they were competing with ARVN and U.S. Army elements for limited assets allocated to those agencies, for example, essential motor transport.[5] These problems might have been dismissed as typical of those which occur in any war were it not that experienced senior officers and headquarters were coming to question the doctrine that the ground forces and civil authority would operate the air request net.

The Air-Ground Request Net

First, it must be noted that not every immediate request requires an immediate response, e.g., in support of troops in contact (TIC). The distinction rather is between preplanned and not preplanned or immediate.[6] Then, in addition, the U.S. Army Special Forces--without artillery and open to attack at any time-- in 1962 and 1963 had their own net. It bypassed division and district and went at once to corps and ASOC. Their request was monitored by their own central station which operated round-the-clock and which alerted the AOC. This arrangement markedly cut reaction time. However, Vietnamese authority came to object.[7]

As noted above, there were parallel military and civilian air request nets below the division/district level. Every level had approval authority. There was no application of the JAGOS principle that the level just below the ASOC, in this case division, would only monitor.* As regards calls from an attacked hamlet or village, which had to call district because it had no link with the military net, that headquarters had 5 options:[8]

        1. Call division.
        2. Do not call division.
        3. Call province.
        4. Decide to call no one.
        5. Decide to wait.

Once a request from a hamlet was in the military net, there was no guarantee it would fare better than a military immediate. Approval authority was very tightly restricted to the corps commander or his chief of staff. They would not delegate and were not

---

*Paragraph 85 b.

always available. Forwarding requests up to them was the task of other officers who might be absent, asleep, disapproving, or most reluctant to relay a request to very senior officers, and then lose face by having it disapproved.

> Not only were ARVN commanders unfamiliar with tactical air power, but they were afraid of it. Furthermore, they did not know how to request air support. They had not been taught how to operate their own Army Air Request Net.[9]

As a result, by 29 November 1962 the operation of the air request net had been identified as the "most outstanding problem" by the Military Assistance Command, Vietnam (MACV). It went on: "Most frequent finding when instances alleging lack of air support investigated (sic) is request did not reach ASOC and attempts to trace responsibility usually fruitless and real reason usually rests within nebulous area cited above." This area had been described as "political, religious, personal or social background and customs of ARVN and civilian officials..."[10] Similar observations were made earlier by Brig. Gen. Gilbert L. Pritchard.[11]

In appraising the effect of air in South Vietnam 1962-1963, observers--including Gen. Curtis E. LeMay, the Air Force Chief of Staff, and Adm. Harry D. Felt, Commander in Chief, Pacific (CINCPAC)--spoke of the non-use of air or its ineffective use. Of all the factors listed by them as contributing to this, the only part of TACS doctrine that was criticized and changed was the air request net.[12]

The New Air Request Net

The first steps to improve the handling of immediate air requests were taken 1 May 1963 when the ARVN and VNAF agreed that immediate air requests would go from battalion--after evaluation at its fire support coordination center (FSCC)--to the corps tactical operation center (TOC) and its collocated ASOC (Figure 5, p 41). Intermediate headquarters would monitor but could not disapprove. When the ASOC received the request, it would deploy a FAC toward the proposed target and alert strike aircraft. When the TOC

IMMEDIATE AIR REQUEST NET

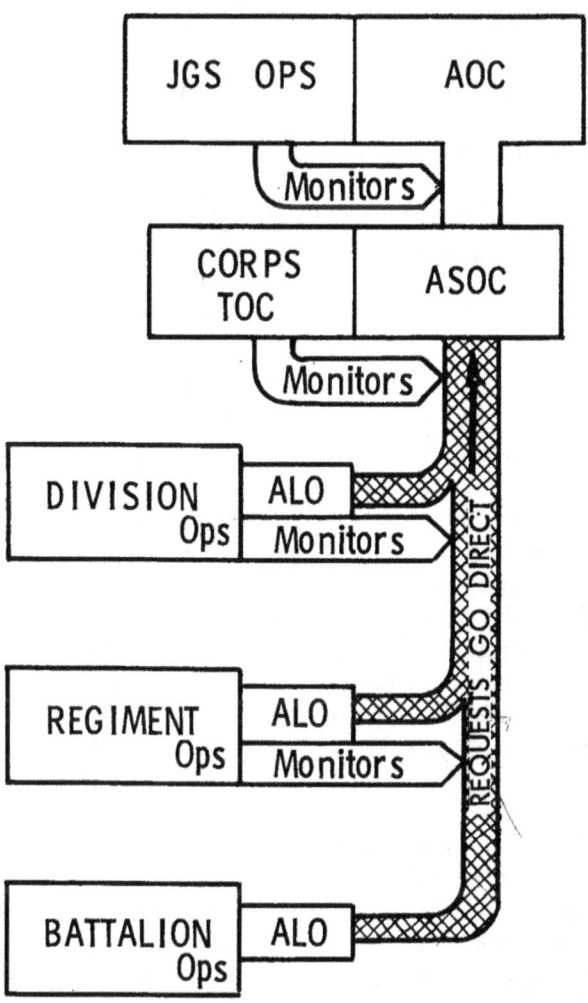

FEATURES:
1. REQUESTS GO DIRECT TO ASOC
2. INTERVENING ECHELONS MONITOR
3. IF NO DISAPPROVALS ARE HEARD IN 5 MINUTES, REQUEST IS CONSIDERED APPROVED.

Figure 5

approved, the ASOC would scramble or divert aircraft. This reflected the recommendation of a combined interservice team of Maj. Gen. Nguyen Khanh, Maj. Gen. Rollen H. Anthis, USAF, and Brig. Gen. Howard K. Eggleston, U.S. Army, who had toured III Corps to find ways to improve the TACS.[13]

Later in 1963 the Air Force Test Unit--Vietnam, which examined the TACS, went farther, recommending sending immediate requests over an Air Force net. The personnel to set up such a net began to arrive early in 1964 as the number of USAF advisory personnel in the TACS increased from 49 to 75.[14]

In May 1964 the new commander of the 2d Air Division, Maj. Gen. Joseph H. Moore, secured the necessary Vietnamese and American approvals to set up a direct air request net manned and operated by airmen. This carried out the Air Force Test Unit's recommendation and, as will be noted, paralleled similar developments in the States. The new direct air request net (DARN) continued the procedure of sending immediates direct from subordinate unit to corps. Each corps was given a net of TACP's with FM, UHF, VHF, and SSB radios. Both VNAF and USAF personnel manned them, with the Air Force providing vehicles and equipment. By 1 December 1964 there were 50 ALO/FAC's, 17 ALO's, and 4 ASOC's, plus the required enlisted personnel. The TACP's were under the ASOC and, as the situation might require (their number was limited), were deployed to regiment or battalion or, in some cases, sector headquarters. Permanent radio stations were established adjacent to division and corps headquarters for monitoring while mobile sets were with the forward command posts. Reception of the DARN was mixed in that not every ARVN division commander liked it. Time and missionary work were needed to persuade.[15]

Developments Within CONUS Affecting Doctrine

In April 1962 Secretary of Defense McNamara ordered the Secretary of the Army to conduct a study of the future of Army aviation without regard to traditional doctrine. The result was the Howze Board report of August 1962. It called for Army air assault divisions with 459 organic aircraft, air cavalry combat brigades, each with 316, and supporting units with organic aircraft on a comparable scale. Submission of the report was followed by a good deal of discussion of roles and missions, as a result of which McNamara ordered the Army and Air Force to examine jointly the question of how to provide better close air support.[16]

The Army and Air Force complied. The 2 boards convened at Fort George G. Meade, Md., and submitted their final report in August 1963. They stated that the JCS had never approved a doctrine for air-ground operations nor for use of the air space over the combat zone. As has been observed, FM 31-35 was a War Department manual, AFM 1-7, Air Force, and JAGOS' originators carefully disclaimed it as joint doctrine. The arrangements of Korea and Vietnam to date had had tacit service approval, not formal JCS action. The boards observed that no joint Army-Air Force agency had a continuing responsibility to examine doctrine and evaluate equipment for CAS. They recommended such an activity.[17]

The board proposals led to the establishment of the USAF Tactical Air Warfare Center (TAWC) 1 November 1963, and plans got under way for joint tests of air-ground doctrine. A series of 3 Indian River test exercises was conducted at Eglin AFB in June-September 1964. These exercises were unilateral in that they were under the new TAWC, though Army elements participated. Their aim was to prepare for the forthcoming U.S. Strike Command (USSTRICOM) tests, Gold Fire.[18]

Held 25 October - 11 November 1964 in the Fort Leonard Wood - Camp Crowder area of Missouri, under a joint task force headquarters, Gold Fire dealt with among other points the direct air request net. To speed the transmission and processing of immediate requests FAC's radioed them direct to a direct air support center (DASC) at corps. Intermediate Army headquarters monitored; their silence indicated approval. This was the DARN General Moore was concurrently installing in South Vietnam. It was also the system Ninth Air Force had used 20 years before in France and Germany in 1944 and which had not attained doctrinal status in the drafting of FM 31-35 because the Army wanted to operate its own air request net.[19]

Formal approval of the DARN by the Air Force and the Army came early in 1965. The Chief of Staff of the Air Force approved 19 March, his Army colleague, 28 April. The Air Force was content to rest on this agreement. It was fully satisfactory and keeping the matter at this stage avoided possible broad interservice complications. The timing of the approval reflected the commitment of large U.S. Army units to Vietnam. The time had come to make the necessary adjustments to smooth the transition from counterinsurgency to large-scale mobile operations by divisions and corps.[20]

Adjusting the Vietnam TACS to Accommodate Large USA/USMC Units*

In describing the impact of the war's new phase on the Vietnam TACS one can present a few generalizations. The basic point is that the commitment of Army and Marine divisions beginning in 1965 compelled corresponding modifications. The Army element in 1966 had to enter the operations centers that the ARVN had left by default. Nomenclature was changed to conform to new Stateside usage. Marine aviation and the B-52's created management problems. The FAC role expanded.

When U.S. forces entered II Corps Tactical Zone (II CTZ) in 1965, they were given their own ASOC which led to parallel DASC's in II CTZ. To the student of World War II and Korea only the parallel control centers (DASC's in contemporary nomenclature) would be a novelty. Very senior and knowledgeable officers differed on the doctrine or management aspects of some of these matters and a brief account following soon after can do no more than record the fact.

In July 1965, Gen. William C. Westmoreland, Commander, U.S. Military Assistance Command, Vietnam (COMUSMACV), was reinforced by the first large Army and Marine units, which

---

*In discussing TACS from 15 August 1965 on, 2 changes in nomenclature to bring SEA usage in line with that developed in CONUS must be noted. The familiar AOC was redesignated a tactical air control center [TACC] and the ASOC's became DASC's.

he then deployed to I Corps along the DMZ, to the Central Highlands, and the sensitive Saigon area. Every maneuver battalion was linked with the TACS by a TACP or its equivalent. The previous month, at his request, the B-52's made their first strike.[21]

General Westmoreland was pleased by the initial work of the Arc Light* force and equally so by the subsequent B-52 operations. As a result, in May 1966 he recommended deploying them so that 6 could attack any target in SEA 7-1/2 hours after MACV's request. In a few months this was being implemented, which in turn raised the question of how their operations would be integrated into the TACS. Looking back on 1961-1966, an Air Force historian has suggested that the position given to the B-52's in the SEA command structure was one of the two major departures from doctrine, that of Marine aviation being the other.[22]

On 23 September 1966, with B-52 operations in full swing, Lt. Gen. William W. Momyer remarked that they had expanded beyond the scope of the original Arc Light system. He thought his Seventh Air Force--now the major Air Force headquarters in South Vietnam--should have operational control during the execution phase, even though MACV continued target selection.[23]

This remark pointed up the varying command channels for control of tactical air established by introduction of the B-52's and Marine aviation. Seventh Air Force was a subordinate command of MACV with "command assignment" over all USAF units based in the Republic of Vietnam. Tactical air units based in Thailand were assigned to the Thirteenth Air Force and under operational control of Seventh Air Force. USMC wings worked directly for Marine ground units and were not available for general use unless released by the Marines. Targets for B-52 strikes were developed by MACV with no inputs or evaluation by Seventh Air Force. The U.S. Navy was also present with three carriers, one of which was striking targets nominated by Seventh Air Force. Therefore, concluded this same historian, there was "no single Air Commander in Vietnam."[24]

---

*Arc Light was the code name for B-52 operations in SEA, initially flown from Guam and Kadena AB, Okinawa; later from Utapao, Thailand.

By 1968, events along the demilitarized zone (DMZ) in the north were acquiring a serious aspect. Looking ahead, General Momyer wrote: "'If the battle at Khe Sanh develops, it may be the event to get the air responsibilities straightened out like we had them in Korea and World War II.'" This paper has documented the practice to which General Momyer referred. His comment was caused in part by the B-52 situation but equally so by the command and control consequences of organic Marine close support aviation.[25]

I Corps Buildup Plus Marine Air Causes Control Problems

In late 1967, an enemy buildup threatening I CTZ became apparent. An Allied buildup followed. Where in April 1967 there had been 58 allied maneuver battalions in I Corps, a year later there were 93, reflecting both the enemy action and its consequent Tet Offensive. In early 1967 there had been no Army battalions present but eventually there were 31.[26]

As Army and ARVN units moved into I Corps, they received close air support from tactical air under I DASC (it will be recalled that DASC's/ASOC's were collocated with corps headquarters). [27] Meanwhile, the 1st Marine Air Wing had its own control system. A separate DASC had been established by MACV for the III Marine Amphibious Force (III MAF), despite the recommendations of the Air Force. The Marines considered that their air assets were organic to the III MAF. Marine requirements had absolute priority and only remaining sorties could be used to meet the needs of others. There were no relative priorities to them. This meant that in South Vietnam sorties were territorially as well as organizationally linked so that sorties allocated to the Marines on, say, 1 November 1966 were 135 of the total 465 available in-country.[28]

The reinforcements continued to move into I Corps and were intermingled with Marine units so that units side-by-side were placing requests with different DASC's. Experience suggested to General Westmoreland that it was not practical to divide I Corps into one zone for Marine aviation, a second for Seventh

Air Force, and a third for carrier air when the enemy had made the battle one continuing action in which Army and Marines fought side by side. "'Obviously [General Momyer] is the man for me to hold responsible for single management of this effort,'" Westmoreland told CINCPAC.[29]

The B-52 effort to support the Marines and ARVN at Khe Sanh also related to the need for single management. Their Operation Niagara added another 2,500 sorties to the 24,400 tactical air strikes flown by USAF, USMC, and USN aircraft in that confined area over a 70-day period. There were also FAC's and gunships. The result was saturated air space so that on occasion strike aircraft could not expend and air lift could not unload. Seventh Air Force, 1st MAW, the Navy carriers, were independently issuing their fragmentary operational orders ("fragging").[30]

On 8 March 1968 COMUSMACV designated his Deputy Commander for Air Operations (Momyer) the single manager for tactical air resources in South Vietnam. Concurrently, he ordered the CG III MAF to place all Marine fixed wing strike and reconnaissance aircraft and their associated air control assets under the new manager's mission direction. Thus, the Commander, Seventh Air Force (also General Momyer) was responsible "for coordinating and directing the tactical air effort throughout South Vietnam..." Putting the tactical air assets in South Vietnam under his mission direction gave him the necessary resources.[31]

"Single Manager" in Operation

The I DASC was expanded to include Marines. A new combined DASC, Victor, would work with the new Provisional Corps, Vietnam, which would control operations in the northern I CTZ. DASC-Victor would be coordinated by I DASC. Each Marine division kept its DASC which, depending on its tactical area of responsibility (TAOR), would be under I DASC or DASC-V. This would comply with COMUSMACV's desire that "'integrity of the Marine tactical control system shall be preserved.'" Marines would be in the MACV ground force element of the TACC

I DASC, and DASC-V. I DASC would serve the CG III MAF. The new single manager, the Commander, Seventh Air Force, exercised operational direction through his TACC at Tan Son Nhut.[32]

The CG III MAF commented that the new organization violated the integrity of the Marine air-ground team which had worked effectively for years. To this, COMUSMACV replied that he had to have more positive control of local air resources and one individual to whom he could turn. Seventh Air Force noted that for a Marine Amphibious Force headquarters to act as a field army headquarters controlling a provisional army corps, as well as its own Marine units, was also a departure from doctrine, yet in the judgment of COMUSMACV the situation required it.[33]

The position of CG III MAF affected the routing of preplanned requests. Requests from the provisional corps which controlled the reinforcements sent to I Corps tactical zone went through III MAF Air. This agency consolidated these requirements with those of the two divisions reinforced which reported directly to CG III MAF with no intervening headquarters. That is, DASC-V passed its requirements to I DASC which processed requests for the entire CTZ.[34]

However, the Marines objected that the single manager system reduced the number of sorties that the Marine ground commander "routinely pre-planned to complement his ground maneuver for the ensuing day..."[35] As a result, beginning 30 May 1968 70 percent of the preplanned sortie capability was allocated to major ground force commanders by weekly frag orders. The decision was made by COMSUMACV. The ground force commanders' "...allocation was almost tantamount to dedicated air, the major difference being that it was subject to withdrawal at any time by [General Momyer] who responded to COMUSMACV guidance." The remaining 30 percent were routed and processed as before on a daily basis (Figure 6, p 50).[36]

Processing the daily preplanned requests was drastically simplified. Previously, 8 items of information had to be given for each request, which were repeated all up the line. The new procedure asked only target description or identification of the supported operation, number of sorties needed, and time over initial point. This greatly reduced the workload.[37]

As the months went by in I CTZ on into 1969, the original simplicity of the direct air request for handling immediates (Figure 7, p 51), was markedly eroded. In many ways, procedures came to resemble those of 1962, for success in large operations made the situation again one of counterinsurgency in many areas of the I CTZ. Thus, even for TIC requests, the first step was to check with the fire support coordination center. If close air support were needed, the request was sent to brigade TACP which passed it to division TACP. If division approved, it went to the DASC. Fighters were not normally scrambled or diverted until political and military clearances were in hand.

Every major element in I Corps handled its immediate requests a bit differently. Thus, the Americal Division requests in southern I CTZ were routed as above. The 1st Marine Division sent its immediates to the Marine DASC which relayed them to the Air Force DASC. In the ARVN, requests came up simultaneously through Air Force and ARVN channels. To be sure that the ARVN I TOC had proper clearances, Air Force DASC duty officers always back-checked. Plainly, the single manager system accommodated these arrangements.[38]

The original charter for the single management system, i.e., the COMUSMACV directive, was still valid in 1969. Since the CG III MAF did not concur in a proposed revision, the MACV chief of staff on 7 February 1969 issued guidance that the existing directive remain in effect.[39]

The Parallel DASC's in II Corps

When major U.S. units entered II CTZ in 1965, they were placed under a newly activated Task Force Alpha,* the Field Force Vietnam headquarters, which was of course promptly given

---

*Not to be confused with the later Task Force Alpha placed in Thailand.

PREPLANNED REQUEST SYSTEM
(Effective 30 May 1968)

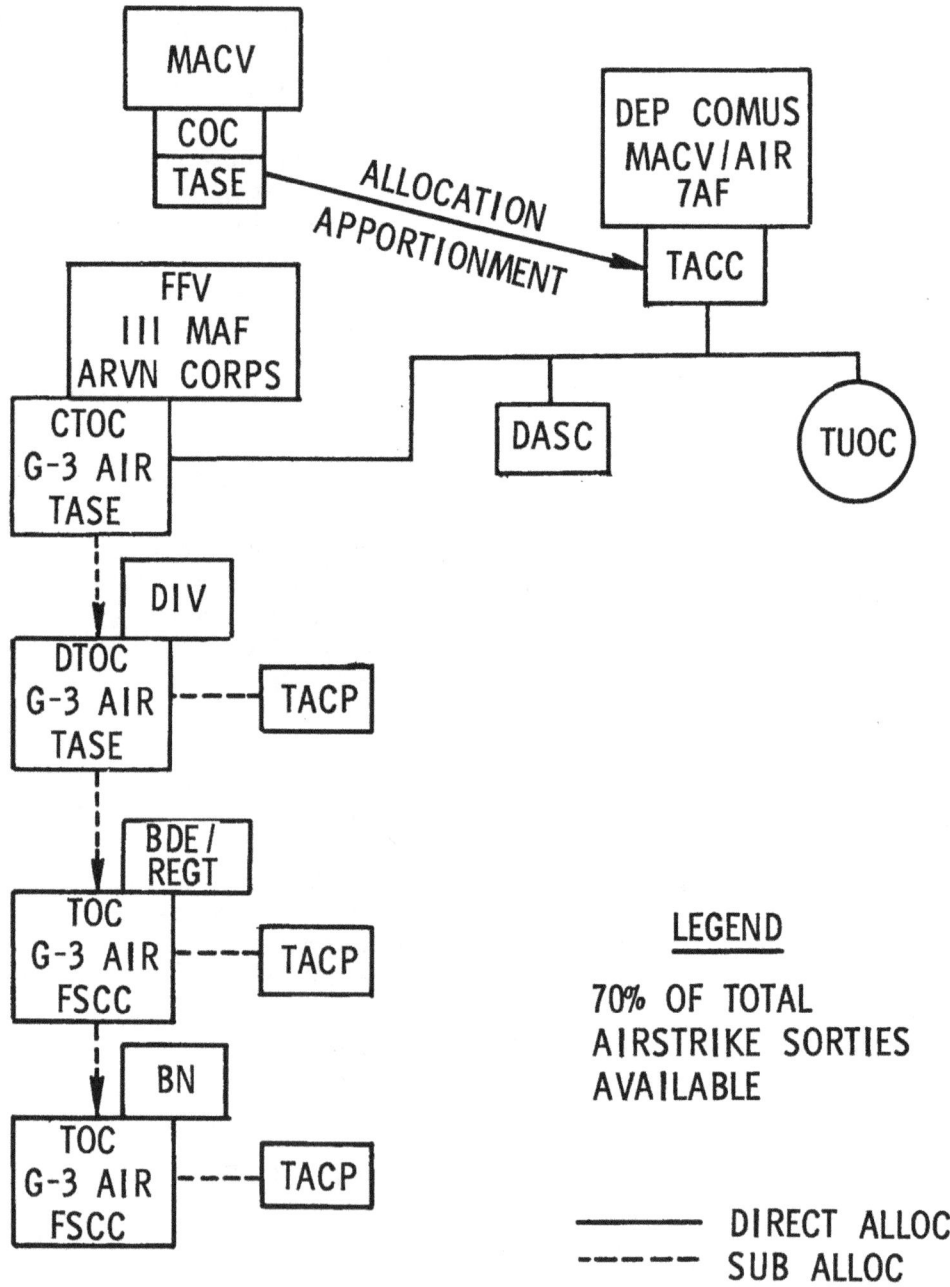

Figure 6

IMMEDIATE AIR REQUESTS

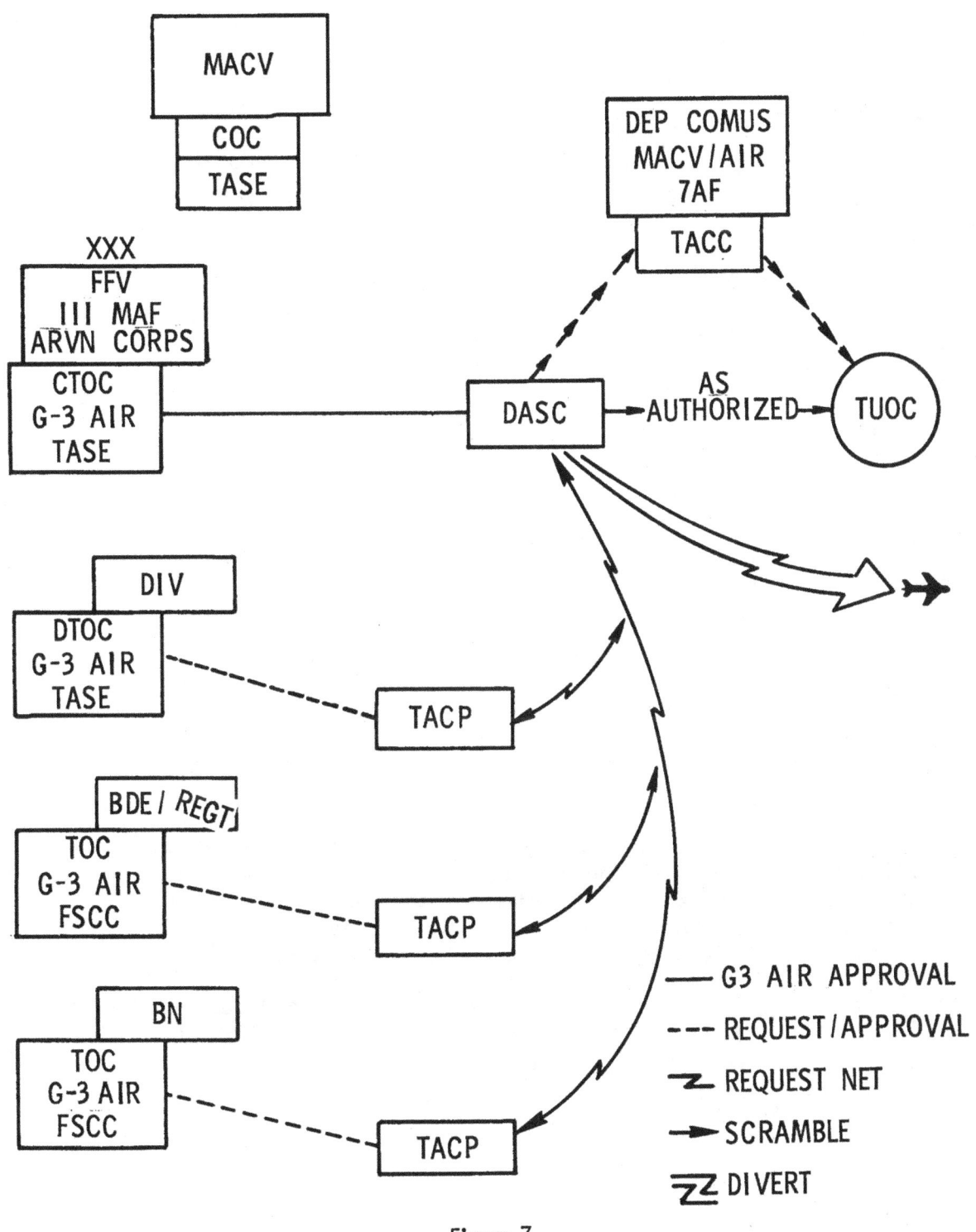

Figure 7

a collocated DASC Alpha. If Free World Military Assistance Forces (FWMAF) acted alone, their close air support came through TACC via DASC Alpha. If they operated with ARVN units, requests were handled by the previously existing II DASC.[40]

The 2 DASC's were not collocated and this caused problems. Finally, on 2 April 1969 all USAF operational elements were placed in DASC Alpha except for a liaison party of one officer and a few airmen at II DASC. TACS elements under the DASC's were also reorganized along national lines. Unhappily, this was believed to have had an adverse effect on the efficiency of the VNAF TACS with the result that by July 1969 50 percent of DASC Alpha's close air support missions were being flown for ARVN units.[41]

Procedures within II Corps for handling immediate requests also came to resemble those of 1962, even as they had in I Corps. Immediates for FWMAF were still sent by the TACP to DASC Alpha over the DARN. However, intermediate echelons had to acknowledge that they had heard the request, and also had to clear.

ARVN immediate requests began with the FAC radioing target data to the Sector TACP. The latter contacted either Sector S-2/3 Air or the TOC duty officer. Sector S-2/3 Air or the TOC duty officer cleared the target with appropriate agencies, e.g., province chief. He then gave the TACP the target number and the names of authorities clearing. Sector TACP then sent the target data to DASC.

Meanwhile, Sector S-2/3 Air or the TOC duty officer warned Division G-3 Air or CTOC duty officer that the request was coming and also passed on its clearance status. Division verified clearance. The action officer obtained any missing clearances and then told corps if the request had or had not been cleared.[42]

Corps then checked the request for clearances and relayed it to the DASC. DASC could neither scramble nor divert until it had been given target number, coordinates, rendezvous point and assurance by Corps G-3 Air or CTOC duty officer that the request had been cleared.[43]

It should not be assumed that the obvious similarity between this system and that of 1962-early 1963 meant that the responsiveness of 1969 was that of earlier years. Project CHECO* personnel believed that one could not evaluate a DASC by checking its response time from computer data banks. They pointed out that the category "immediate request" referred simply to requests that were not preplanned. The adjective "immediate" should not lead to the conclusion that all such requests were TIC or ASAP.

The consensus of responsible officers in the II CTZ TACS was that it was "effective and highly responsive," that response to troops in contact was "timely and rapid."[44]

The FAC's Roles and Missions Expand, 1965-1969

The officer in IV Corps DASC who remarked, "'The FAC is, at the same time, a politician, administrative officer, radio operator, and an effective weapons controller'" showed how counterinsurgency and the wide deployment of small units had added to the FAC's duties since FM 31-35 was published in 1946. Then, the missions of weapons controller and radio operator were clearly implied in its paragraph 45.[45] Politician and administrator were not. Headquarters, Pacific Air Force (PACAF) pointed out that the duties assumed by FAC's in Southeast Asia far outran the limits envisaged by AFR 20-23, 16 April 1965, under which they were trained. In effect, they were local Air Force representatives and so their advice and assistance paralleled the air effort in SEA. Airlift, reconnaissance, psychological warfare, and on occasion medical evacuation and civic action were among their responsibilities. So far as PACAF was aware in 1971, this had yet to be reflected in any doctrinal publication.[46]

Classes of FAC's and area assignments were also new developments. Area assignments have been mentioned above, but they were not formalized until 1 September 1967. Then, an ALO and several FAC's were provided to sectors in division

---

*Contemporary Historical Evaluation of Current Operations.

tactical zones. "Following that development, the regiments were normally supported by the FAC's whose assigned province they were operating in."[47]

The FAC's with area assignments were Class C FAC's. They had had O-1 aircraft checkout, air-ground school, and FAC training. Four to 6 of them were assigned to each province, with ALO's each at ARVN divisions and corps. They became intimately familiar with every aspect of the local situation, the terrain, enemy order of battle, local activity patterns, and were air advisers to the province chiefs. They did a great deal of visual reconnaissance. The ALO wrote the efficiency reports for his associated FAC's and, in effect, was their commander, even though the tactical air support group gave logistical, personnel, and administrative support.[48]

The Class A FAC's were Air Force fighter pilots and worked only with U.S. Army units. They controlled close air support of the classic sort as discussed above.[49]

An example of the FAC as ALO and air adviser to the small unit commander is the work of the Barky FAC's in I Corps in 1969. Barky FAC's were assigned to the 1st Brigade, 5th Infantry Division (Mechanized) but could be expected to help any unit in the 3d Marine Division's area of responsibility. They knew the area well and, on arriving over a company, they would discuss the situation with the company commander and agree with him on the use of preplanned or immediate strikes that day. Agreement reached, the FAC would then initiate action to clear and coordinate necessary strikes by asking both DASC and the ground commander to clear the grid square. Since FAC's rotated in 2-hour intervals, plainly there would be some repetition of this process.[50]

The FAC could also adjust artillery. There were procedures for coordinating artillery fires before, during, and after air strikes (combat reporting centers had current information on artillery activity and alerted strike aircraft) but, with all the FAC had to do, a Project CHECO historian thought he found this coordination with artillery to be complicated. However, the FAC could and would handle both artillery and strike aircraft.

Thus, on 27 June 1969 Barky FAC Capt. R.C. Merkle coordinated Marine F-4's and UH-1 gunships, an armed Marine OV-10, and 30 minutes of artillery fires to help defend a 1/5 Mechanized Division command post in a 3-hour successful engagement.[51]

Command and Control of CAS Affects a Battle: Duc Lap, 1968

Special Forces in the field had no TACP's. When a FAC learned of a target involving them he passed it on to his TACP while the Special Forces commander obtained clearances from the Vietnamese officials concerned. "The problem became extremely complex when a Special Forces camp was under siege. When it occurred, elements of several different forces flooded into the area." Of necessity, an ad hoc local DASC had to be set up with representatives of all elements involved.[52] This was done at Duc Lap Special Forces Camp, 23 August-8 September 1968.

Duc Lap is in a hilly, jungle area about 5 kilometers from the Cambodian border and 25 kilometers from Ban Me Thuot along Route 14. Avenues of approach from Cambodia are numerous. About 4,000 North Vietnamese soldiers of the North Vietnamese 1st Army division, averaging about 25 years of age, and with 9-13 months training, well-equipped and in good physical condition, attacked a small complex of installations at Duc Lap. The defenders were largely paramilitary, a group of 12 companies reinforced by 2 battalions of ARVN regulars. Montagnards, Vietnamese, and Americans were all present and working together. The enemy had been able to build firing positions within range of the Special Forces camp and had the advantage of surprise. His forces were all regulars and outnumbered the defenders throughout the action. The combination of surprise and loosely organized heterogenous defenders is a classic recipe for disaster but the defenders had the trump card of well-managed, massive close air support.

The attack began 23 August and triggered immediate air support. Direction of the air battle was assumed by the ALO, Lt. Col. Charles N. Harrison, who controlled the air resources of Darlac and Quang Duc Provinces through the TACP of the ARVN 23d Infantry Division. With great foresight and disregarding an optimistic intelligence report, the division commander, Gen. Trung Quan An, Col. Rex R. Sage, U.S. Army, his senior adviser, and Colonel Harrison had set up an operations center with the TACP, U.S. Army G-3, G-3 Air, ARVN G-3 air, VNAF, the Artillery Adviser, and Intelligence.

During the first day the ALO appreciated that 4 different target areas were involved, that the enemy force though large was probably not of division strength. He therefore directed that 2 FAC's be airborne at all times in the area; after 24 August, he had a set of fighters arriving every 20-25 minutes. FAC's appeared at first light and stayed until night-flying gunships could take over.

Initially, only the 2 local province FAC's were allowed to direct strikes. Replacement was made possible by having the incoming FAC overlap for an hour's listening to transmissions and studying the situation. This was done until reinforcing FAC's were thoroughly oriented.

Two FAC's had primary duties in the control center, 6 were primary FAC's, one primarily did visual reconnaissance of Darlac Province, and other FAC's could reinforce from the 2d Brigade, U.S. 4th Division. FAC duties included:

> Coordinating with as many as 5 commanders, up to regiment and subsector.
> Keeping track of the ground situation.
> Adjusting artillery.
> Directing gunships.
> Helping in all aspects of helicopter landings.
> Coordinating with other FAC's when such were present and directing strikes.
> Acting as relay stations.
> Covering downed aircraft.
> Normal strike direction duties.

There were 392 sorties by tactical air between 23-29 August. These in turn included about 3,300 passes. They were controlled by FAC's who also controlled over 100 gunship sorties, adjusted or cleared artillery fire more than 50 times, and directed fire suppression for 6 helilifts. They flew at night and in thunderstorms, including 13 night strikes in marginal weather.

Fighting around the Duc Lap Special Forces Camp was over on the night of the 25th, save for sporadic mortaring until the night of the 27th. Fighting around a subsector headquarters continued until the 29th when the outcome was no longer in doubt, although contact continued into September. As of 9 September, friendly personnel killed in action (KIA) totalled 117, the enemy, 839.

Aerial ordnance expended included 581,000 lbs. of bombs, 485,000 lbs. of napalm, 200,000 lbs. of cluster bomb units (CBU's), plus 1,140 rockets and 36,000 rounds of ammunition.

The friendly forces which received this support included 12 companies plus 2 platoons of paramilitary forces and 2 battalions of ARVN infantry, under command and control of 23d Division headquarters. They numbered about 2,500 men. They defended a Special Forces camp, a scout camp, a subsector headquarters and an outpost, or were maneuvering in from a landing zone.

Looking back on the defense of Duc Lap, the Senior Army Adviser, Colonel Sage, mentioned the coordination of close air support as a significant factor: [53]

> I've never seen closer cooperation between the Tac Air and Ground Forces than was exhibited at Duc Lap and I think that is one reason it is still in existence and under Allied control today. Had it not been for the job done by Tac Air and by the Spooky [gunship] operations at night, I'm sure this outpost would have gone down and also the Subsector as well as the Scout outpost. The coordination which was effected here at our headquarters in supporting the operation by Tac Air was primarily carried on by our ALO. He and his FAC's worked day and night in supporting the operation and did a truly outstanding job. I've never seen better performance by any portion of the Armed Forces.

SUMMARY

Close air support was introduced by the Royal Flying Corps in the Battle of Cambrai in November 1917. Unified control of air and exploitation of its mobility were accepted RFC principles a year earlier. Brig. Gen. William Mitchell appreciated these principles and incorporated them into U.S. practice at St. Mihiel and in the Meuse-Argonne, 1918.

The sensational German victories of 1939-1940 demonstrated the necessity of an independent, co-equal air force and the effectiveness of massed tactical air power under central control quickly responding to the combat situation. The U.S. armed forces sought to adjust their organization and doctrines accordingly and test their innovations in combat. The process took several years.

An attempt to parcel out tactical air among "support commands," one per army corps, proved unworkable in Tunisia in the winter of 1942-1943. It was replaced by a tactical air force, centrally controlled, and cooperating with, rather than controlled by, the ground forces. This became doctrine in 1943. The next problem, that of interface with the ground combat units so that air could quickly and effectively respond to requests from infantry and armor, was solved in the field 1943-1944.

During 1944, in Italy, Burma, France, and the Pacific, there were to be found collocated air-ground headquarters, tactical air control parties, continual joint planning by ground and air intelligence and operations officers, and tactical air controllers. When airborne, as they were on occasion in Italy, Burma, and France, the officers were forward air controllers in all but name.

In 1945, the practices of World War II were published as doctrine in FM 31-35, Air-Ground Operations. FM 31-35 provided a complete tactical air control system, with its components of collocated air and ground headquarters, a joint operations center including a tactical air control center, tactical air control parties, forward air controllers, and air liaison officers. During the Korean War 1950-1953, this Tactical Air Control System was soon installed and close air support became fully effective and a critical factor in defending South Korea. In the last month of the conflict the air request net was modified in that the Air Force and the Army agreed the latter would supply both equipment and enlisted personnel for tactical air control parties, the Air Force, the forward air controller.

In the 1950's the Army's desire for organic aviation and the steady improvement of computers and their peripheral equipment had some impact on publications of doctrinal nature, though the Joint Chiefs of Staff took no stand. Thus, the latest text (September 1957) ended the joint operations center in that the ground force element became a separate tactical support center. This in turn controlled army aviation. Each field army was given a mobile air support operations center, a forward agency of what had been the air component of the air operations center. This was the state of doctrine in January 1962 when the U.S. Air Force installed a TACS in South Vietnam.

In South Vietnam, the Air Force had a dual mission--training the South Vietnamese and supporting them. The TACS in 1962-1965 reflected this. USAF air liaison officers and forward air controllers had to be deployed in the absence of qualified Vietnamese Army ground officers. The forwarding and processing of immediate air requests was unacceptably slow and uncertain. Finally, in 1963-1964 Vietnamese and U.S. authority agreed that immediate requests would go directly from requester to corps with intermediate headquarters monitoring, and that the air request net would be manned and operated by airmen. This was a return to World War II practice.

When both sides committed infantry divisions in 1965, the TACS had to adjust accordingly. For a time, the use of B-52's and the presence of U.S. Marine Corps aviation led to a weakening of the principle of unified control. Then, the Communist offensive of early 1968 led COMUSMACV, Gen. William C. Westmoreland, to make the Seventh Air Force commander, Lt. Gen. William W. Momyer, his "single manager" for air.

Throughout these years the growth in versatility and responsibility of the forward air controller was marked. His activities in advising and assisting lower level military and civilian authority came to parallel the range of USAF activities in South Vietnam.

Examining tactical air control in 4 wars, World Wars I and II, Korea, and Vietnam, and the experience of 3 nations, Great Britain, Germany, and the United States, suggests that the principles of tactical air control are independent of nationality and terrain, and largely so of technology. Sensors and computers may permit automating many of the procedures involved, but changes in procedure should not be confused with changes in doctrine.

FOOTNOTES

Part I

1. Hilary St. George Saunders, *Per Ardua; The Rise of British Air Power, 1911-1939* (London, 1939), pp 85-86, Ch 11, 166-69, 261, 264, 269. Its explicit treatment of doctrine and its evolution makes this a most important book. For a more detailed treatment of early experiments in close air support of armor, see J.F.C. Fuller, *Tanks in the Great War*, 1914-1918 (New York, 1920), Ch XXXII.

2. *Final Report of Chief of Air Service, AEF*, in Rprt of CINC, AEF, Staff Sections and Services (Washington, D.C., 1948), p 230.

3. Hist Div, DA, *U.S. Army in the World War, 1917-1919*. Meuse-Argonne Operations of the AEF (Washington, 1948), p 48; William Mitchell, *Memoirs of World War I* (New York, 1960), Chs 29, 31, 32, p 261.

4. Gen. der Fl. a. d. Paul Deichmann, *German Air Force Operations in Support of the Army* (USAF Historical Study No. 163) (Maxwell AFB, Ala., Jun 62), pp 130-32. Hereafter cited Deichmann, *GAF Operations*.

5. A. Goutard, *The Battle of France, 1940* (New York, 1959), p 145 (hereafter cited Goutard, *Battle of France*); Alistair Horne, *To Lose a Battle, France 1940* (Boston, 1949), pp 288-306, 333, 437. Hereafter cited Horne, *To Lose a Battle*.

6. Deichmann, *GAF Operations*, p 140; Horne, *To Lose a Battle*, pp 162-63.

7. Air Ministry Pamphlet No. 428, *The Rise and Fall of the German Air Force* (1933 to 1945) London: Air Ministry, 1948). Pp 42-43 describe Luftwaffe doctrine, 1939-1940.

8. Deichmann, *GAF Operations*, pp 16, 17, 30-32, 42, 79, 130-32, 136, 138.

9. Horne, To Lose a Battle, pp 116, 120, 121, 436-37; Guide Michelin, France, 1969.

10. Horne, To Lose a Battle, p 437; Goutard, Battle of France, p 36.

11. Robert Frank Futrell, Ideas, Concepts, Doctrine; A History of Basic Thinking in the United States Air Force 1907-1964 (Air University, 1971), p 113. Hereafter cited Futrell, Ideas, Concepts, Doctrine. This is the basic source for USAF doctrine.

12. Ibid., p 116.

13. Ibid., p 117; Wesley Frank Craven and James Lea Cate, eds, The Army Air Forces in World War II, vol II, Europe-Torch to Pointblank, August 1942 to December 1943 (Chicago, 1956), p 137 (hereafter cited Craven and Cate, II); FM 31-35, Aviation in Support of Ground Forces, 9 April 1942. Paragraph 37d has the proviso on final decision.

14. FM 31-35, 9 April 1942, paras 7-9, 37.

15. See entries under "maneuvers" in index to Mark Skinner Watson, Chief of Staff: Prewar Plans and Preparation (Washington, D. C., 1950).

16. Forrest C. Pogue, George C. Marshall: Ordeal and Hope (New York, 1966) p 164.

17. Ibid., pp 162, 164.

18. Futrell, Ideas, Concepts, Doctrine, pp 116-119.

19. Craven and Cate, IV, The Pacific-Guadalcanal to Saipan, August 1942 to July 1944. (Chicago) p 41; Lt. Col. Frank O. Hough, USMCR, Maj. Verle E. Ludwig, USMC, Henry I. Shaw, Jr., Pearl Harbor to Guadalcanal, Vol I, History of Marine Corps Operations in World War II. (Hqs USMC, Washington, D. C. n.d.) pp 19, 298.

20. Craven and Cate, IV, p 97.

Notes to pages 10-17

21. Louis Morton, *Strategy and Command: The First Two Years* (Washington, D.C. 1962) pp 257-261. The last sentence closely paraphrases one on page 259.

22. *Ibid.*, p 263.

23. Futrell, *Ideas, Concepts, Doctrine*, p 121; (2) Craven and Cate, II, p 138.

24. Craven and Cate, II, p 140.

25. *Ibid.*, p 165 and fn 77.

26. Lt. Col. James L. Cash, "The Employment of Air Power in the North African Campaign," unpublished Ms (C), dated 9 Oct 51, pp 22-23; Craven and Cate, II, pp 153-57.

27. Cash Ms cited above, p 24.

28. Craven and Cate, II, pp 161-65.

29. *Ibid.*, p 164.

30. George F. Howe, *Northwest Africa: Seizing the Initiative in the West* (Washington, D.C., 1957), p 673.

31. Futrell, *Ideas, Concepts, Doctrine*, pp 121-22.

32. FM 100-20, 21 July 1943, III, 14d, 16.

33. Futrell, *Ideas, Concepts, Doctrine*, p 126.

34. Craven and Cate, IV, pp 165-66, 182, 188, 340.

35. *Ibid.*, p 343.

36. Futrell, *Ideas, Concepts, Doctrine*, p 161.

37. *Ibid.*, p 162.

38. Charles F. Romanus and Riley Sunderland, *Stilwell's Command Problems* (Washington, D.C. 1956) p 89.

39. Craven and Cate, Vol III, Europe: Argument to V-E Day, January 1944 to May 1945. (Chicago, 1951) p 208.

40. Martin H. Blumenson, Breakout and Pursuit (Department of the Army, Washington, D.C. 1961), pp 220-223, 229, 232-33. Hereafter cited Blumenson, Breakout and Pursuit. Weather caused the cancellation.

41. Ibid., pp 245-46.

42. Craven and Cate, III, pp 238-240, 242.

43. Ibid., p 270.

44. Futrell, Ideas, Concepts, Doctrine, pp 126, 132, 165.

45. Ibid., pp 132, 189.

46. Ibid., pp 278, 339-341.

47. Ibid., pp 339-341, 346-47.

48. Robert Frank Futrell, The United States Air Force in Korea 1950-1953 (New York, 1961) pp 658-662. Hereafter cited Futrell, Korea.

49. Ibid., pp 315-16.

50. Ibid., pp 7-14, 22-28; (Roy E. Appleman, South to the Naktong, North to the Yalu (Washington, D.C. 1961) p 477. Hereafter cited Appleman.

51. Futrell, Korea, pp 75-78.

52. Ibid., pp 81-82.

53. Appleman, p 477.

54. Futrell, Korea, pp 661-663; Futrell, Ideas, Concepts, Doctrine, pp 279-281.

55. Futrell, Korea, p 661.

Notes to pages 32-39   65

56. Futrell, Ideas, Concepts, Doctrine, pp 371, 742.

57. Ibid., pp 357-359. The passage above compresses, in order to stay within the scope of the paper.

58. Futrell, Korea, p 660, discusses the operational problems caused by night and bad weather.

59. Futrell, Ideas, Concepts, Doctrine, pp 374, 742.

60. Ibid., p 743. For an example of the Typhoons at work, see Blumenson, Breakout and Pursuit, p 474 on the action at Mortain.

61. Futrell, Ideas, Concepts, Doctrine, pp 744-45.

Part II

1. HQS, PACAF, SecDef Book for Jan Mtg, 15 Jan 62, Sec II, Tab 3-B.

2. Hist, 2d ADVON, 15 Nov 61-8 Oct 62, pp 89-95; Ltr, HQS PACAF to HQ USAF (Off/AF Hist) subj: Draft History 3 Aug 71.

3. Draft presentation, Anthis for Mar 62 SecDef Conf. "Air Operations" (SD-203); Hist, 2d ADVON, Nov 61-Oct 62; Hist, 2d AirDiv, Jan-Jun 64, pp 73-75; Ltr, Lt. Col. Charles D. Easely, 2JOC, to 2ODC, subj: Deficiencies in the TACS, c. 1 Jul 62.

4. Msg, MAC J3 5075 MACV to CINCPAC, 290720Z.

5. Ltr, PACAF to Off/AF Hist, 3 Aug 71, p 4.

6. Ernie S. Montagliani and Capt John R. Wohnsigl, The DASCs in II CTZ, Jul 65-Jun 69 (HQ PACAF, Project CHECO, 31 Aug 69), p 27 (hereafter cited Montagliani and Wohnsigl).

7. Maj. Ralph Rowley, USAF FAC Operations in Southeast Asia, 1961-1965 (Off/AF Hist, Jan 72), p 67, (hereafter cited Rowley, FAC Operations).

8. Hq, 2d Air Div, Ops Analysis Memo No. 2, "Air Request System and Supporting Communications," 27 Oct 62.

9. Warren A. Trest, *Control of Air Strikes in SEA, 1961-1966* (HQ PACAF, Project CHECO, 1 Mar 66), p 10 (hereafter cited Trest, *Control of Air Strikes*); Rowley, *FAC Operations*, pp 62-67.

10. Msg, MAC J3 5075, MACV to CINCPAC, 290720Z Nov 62.

11. Brig Gen Gilbert L. Pritchard, Rprt of Visit, 9-27 Jul 62-1 Aug 62.

12. Admiral Felt is quoted in Hist, 2d Air Div, Jan-Jun 64, p 71; Rprt of CSAF's Visit to SVN, Apr 62; Msg, MACV to CINCPAC, info 2AD, 161041Z May 62; Ltr, Maj Hal G. Bowers, ALO 5th ARVN Div to DD III ASOC, subj: Oct 62 ALO Activities Rprt, 16 Nov 62.

13. Rowley, *FAC Operations*, pp 61, 69-70; General Anthis commanded the 2d Air Division.

14. Ibid., pp 69-70; Hist, 2d Air Div, Jan-Jun 64, p 75.

15. Trest, *Control of Air Strikes*, pp 17-18, 36-37; ltr, PACAF to Off/AF Hist, 3 Aug 71, p 5.

16. Futrell, *Ideas, Concepts, Doctrine*, pp 747-48.

17. Ibid., pp 749-750.

18. Ibid., p 753.

19. Ibid.

20. Rprt, Alfred Goldberg and Lt. Col. Donald Smith, *Army-Air Force Relations: The Close Air Support Issue* (RAND Corp., 1971) p 24; Intvw, author with Lt. Col. Ellis C. Vander Pyl, Jr., Dir/Doctrine, Concepts, and Objectives, HQ USAF, 17 Jan 72.

21. Adm. U.S.G. Sharp and Gen. W.C. Westmoreland, *Report on the War in Vietnam* (Washington, 1968), p 98.

22. Trest, *Control of Air Strikes*, pp 41-42, 88-89.

23. Ibid., pp 88-89.

24. Ibid., pp 82-83.

25. Gen. Momyer's remark is in a MR quoted in Lt. Col. Robert M. Burch, Single Manager for Air in SVN (HQ PACAF, Project CHECO, 18 Mar 69), p 3 (hereafter cited Burch, Single Manager).

26. Warren A. Trest, Single Manager for Air in SVN (HQ PACAF, Project CHECO, 1 Jul 68), pp 4-6 (hereafter cited Trest, Single Manager).

27. Ibid., p 10.

28. Trest, Control of Air Strikes, p 84.

29. Trest, Single Manager, pp 10, 15-16.

30. Ibid., pp 10-11.

31. Ibid., vi, I.

32. Ibid., pp 21-22.

33. Ibid., pp 31-32.

34. Ibid., fig 7, p 23.

35. Burch, Single Manager, p 52.

36. Lt. Col. Thomas D. Wade, Seventh Air Force Tactical Control Center Operations (HQ PACAF, Project CHECO, 18 Oct 68), pp 14-16.

37. Ibid., p 16.

38. Capt. Kenneth J. Alnwick, Direct Air Support in I Corps, July 1965-June 1969 (HQ PACAF, Project CHECO, 31 Aug 69), pp 34-37 (hereafter cited Alnwick, Direct Air Support).

39. Burch, Single Manager, p 54.

40. Montagliani and Wohnsigl, p 4.

41. Ibid., pp 4-5.

42. Ibid., p 15.

43. Ibid., pp 13-14.

44. Ibid., p 27.

45. Trest, Control of Air Strikes, p 48.

46. Ltr, PACAF to Off/AF Hist, 3 Aug 71, pp 6-7.

47. Ibid., p 6.

48. Trest, Control of Air Strikes, p 46; Rowley, FAC Operations, p 99; Maj James B. Overton, FAC Operations in Close Support Role in SVN, (HQ PACAF, Project CHECO, 21 Jan 69), p 8.

49. Trest, Control of Air Strikes, p 46.

50. Alnwick, Direct Air Support, p 67.

51. Ibid., pp 68-70.

52. Ibid., pp 35-36.

53. Two sources were used for this sketch of TACS at Duc Lap: AAR, 23d Div (ARVN) USAF TACP, "The Battle of Duc Lap, 23 Aug-8 Sep 68"; AAR, 21st Mil Hist Det, 5th Spl Forces Gp, 1st Spl Forces, 27 Nov 68.

GLOSSARY OF TERMS AND ABBREVIATIONS

AAF	Army Air Forces
AAR	After Action Report
ADCOM	Advanced Echelon, Far East Command
AFEO	Air Force Eyes Only
AFF	Army Field Forces
AFM	Air Force manual
AGF	Army Ground Forces
ALO	air liaison officer
AOC	air operations center
ARVN	Army of the Republic of Vietnam
ASAP	as soon as possible
ASF	Army Service Forces
ASOC	Air Support Operations Center
ASP	air support party
CAS	close air support
CINC	Commander in Chief
CINCPAC	Commander in Chief, Pacific
COMUSMACV	Commander, U.S. Military Assistance Command, Vietnam
CONARC	Continental Army Command
CONUS	Continental United States
CP	command post
CTOC	corps tactical operations center
CTZ	corps tactical zone
DARN	direct air request net
DASC	direct air support center
Div	division
DMZ	demilitarized zone
ETO	European Theater of Operations

FAC	Forward Air Controller
FEAF	Far East Air Forces
FM	frequency modulation; field manual
FSCC	fire support coordination center
FWMAF	Free World Military Assistance Forces
G-1	Personnel section of divisional or higher staff
G-2	Intelligence section
G-3	Operations section
G-4	Supply section
JAGOS	Joint Air Ground Operations
JCS	Joint Chiefs of Staff
JOC	Joint Operations Center
JTD	Joint Training Directive
MAAG	Military Assistance Advisory Group
MACV	Military Assistance Command, Vietnam
MAF	Marine Amphibious Force
MAW	Marine Air Wing
MR	Memorandum for Record
OPD	Operations Division
PACAF	Pacific Air Forces
RAF	Royal Air Force
RFC	Royal Flying Corps
ROK	Republic of Korea
SOP	Standard Operating Procedure
SPA	South Pacific Area
SSB	single sideband
SVN	South Vietnam

TAC	Tactical Air Command
TACP	tactical air control party
TACS	tactical air control system
TADC	tactical air direction center
TAOR	tactical area of responsibility
TAWC	Tactical Air Warfare Center
TIC	troops in contact
TOC	tactical operations center
TSC	tactical support center
UHF	ultra high frequency
USAAF	United States Army Air Forces
USMC	United States Marine Corps
USN	United States Navy
VHF	very high frequency
VNAF	Vietnamese Air Force

www.ingramcontent.com/pod-product-compliance
Lightning Source LLC
Chambersburg PA
CBHW080525110426
42742CB00017B/3242